DIETER SCHWARZ

Gerhard Richter

Two Grey Double Mirrors for a Pendulum in Münster

2018

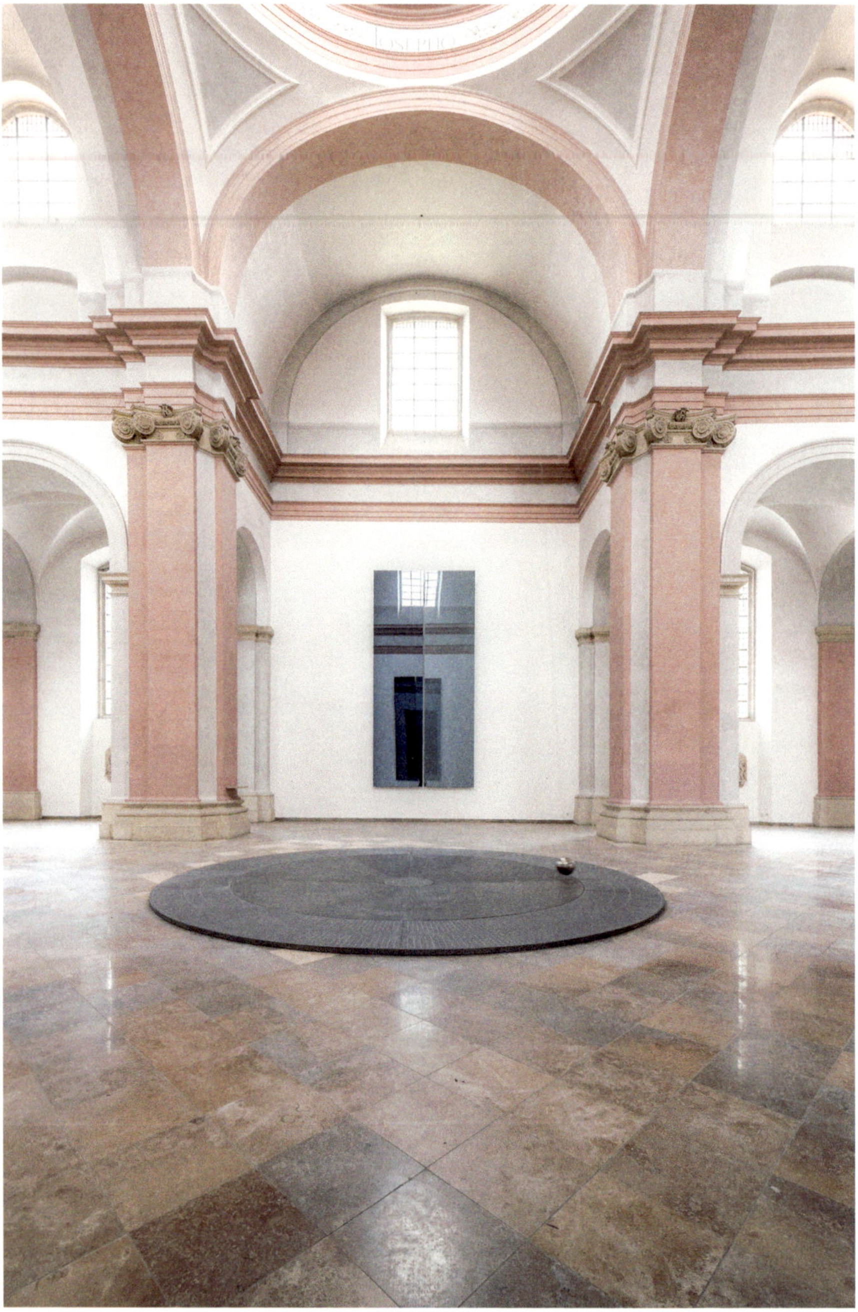

DIETER SCHWARZ

Gerhard Richter

Two Grey Double Mirrors for a Pendulum in Münster

2018

GERHARD RICHTER ARCHIV
STAATLICHE KUNSTSAMMLUNGEN
DRESDEN

VERLAG DER BUCHHANDLUNG
WALTHER UND FRANZ KÖNIG, KÖLN

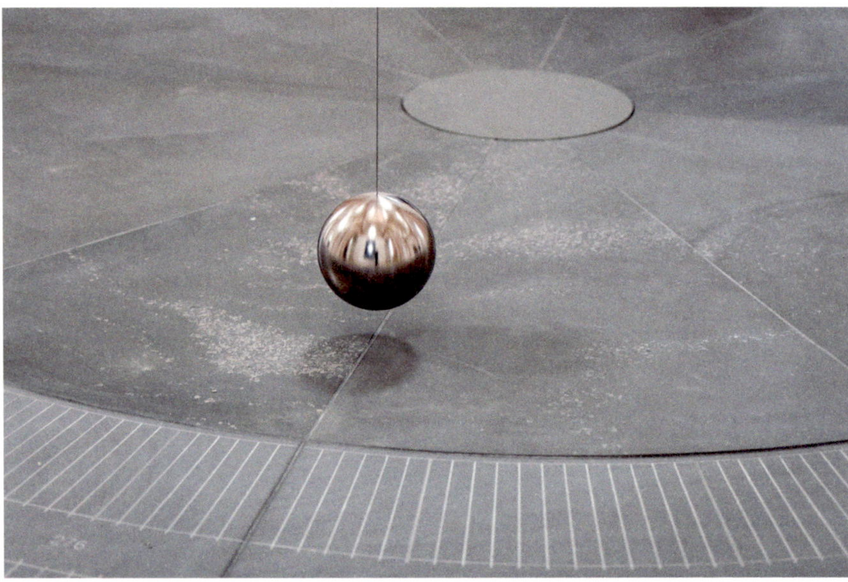

Contents

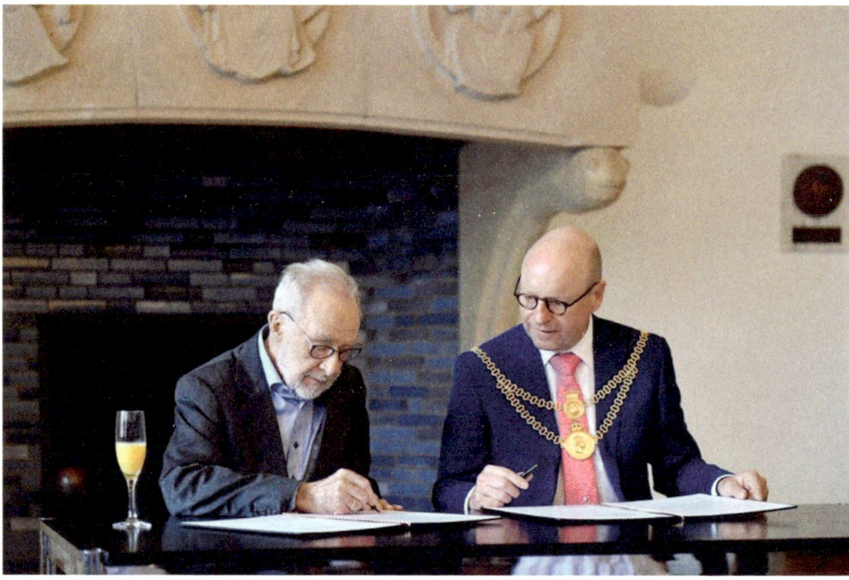

FIG. 1

Gerhard Richter and Lord Mayor
Markus Lewe signing the art donation agreement,
30 November 2017

A Victory for Science

On 17 June 2018 a new work by Gerhard Richter was inaugurated in the Dominican Church (Dominikanerkirche) in Münster, which is now home to this gift from the artist to the city. As the title implies, this is a multipart work consisting of a Foucault pendulum suspended from the dome, a specifically calculated plane of oscillation, and two pairs of grey mirrors fixed to the side walls. This extraordinary, special ensemble is one of the few works by Gerhard Richter made for a specific location and on permanent view in that location. In that sense it is a counterpart to the pavilion on the island of Toyoshima in Japan's Seto Inland Sea completed just a few years earlier, in 2015, where Richter – with similar rigor – matched the work of art to both its purpose-built home and its natural environment.

It is not just the rare unity of a work and its surroundings that is of particular interest here, it is also the fact that this ensemble of distinctly different elements – possibly a surprising combination for many viewers – in fact brings together motifs that have a long history in Richter's oeuvre – a given (in this case the pendulum), glass and reflections, monochromaticism (in particular the colour grey), and a monumental spatial composition. And, last but not least, the utilization of a pendulum gives the work programmatic significance. "'An installation of this kind is not just beautiful,' as Richter said in this Baroque church on a busy shopping street in Münster, 'it is also fascinating for the way it moves.' The fact that a pendulum of this kind once dispelled medieval misconceptions of the shape and movement of the Earth makes the church a particularly interesting location for him. 'It is decisive proof of the rotation of our planet – a victory for science.'"[1]

---

1 "Gerhard Richter installiert Pendel in Münsters Dominikanerkirche," *Kirche + Leben* (Netz), 30 November 2017. In his address on the deconsecration of the church, Stefan Zekorn, auxiliary bishop in the Diocese of Münster, did not miss the opportunity to respond to Richter's comment. He pointed out that if everything is in motion and is relative, then this can only be demonstrated in relation to a fixed point, the suspension point, and in his view faith fulfils the same function as that point. (Auxiliary Bishop Stefan Zekorn to Gerhard Richter, Münster, 5 December 2017; Gerhard Richter Archive.)

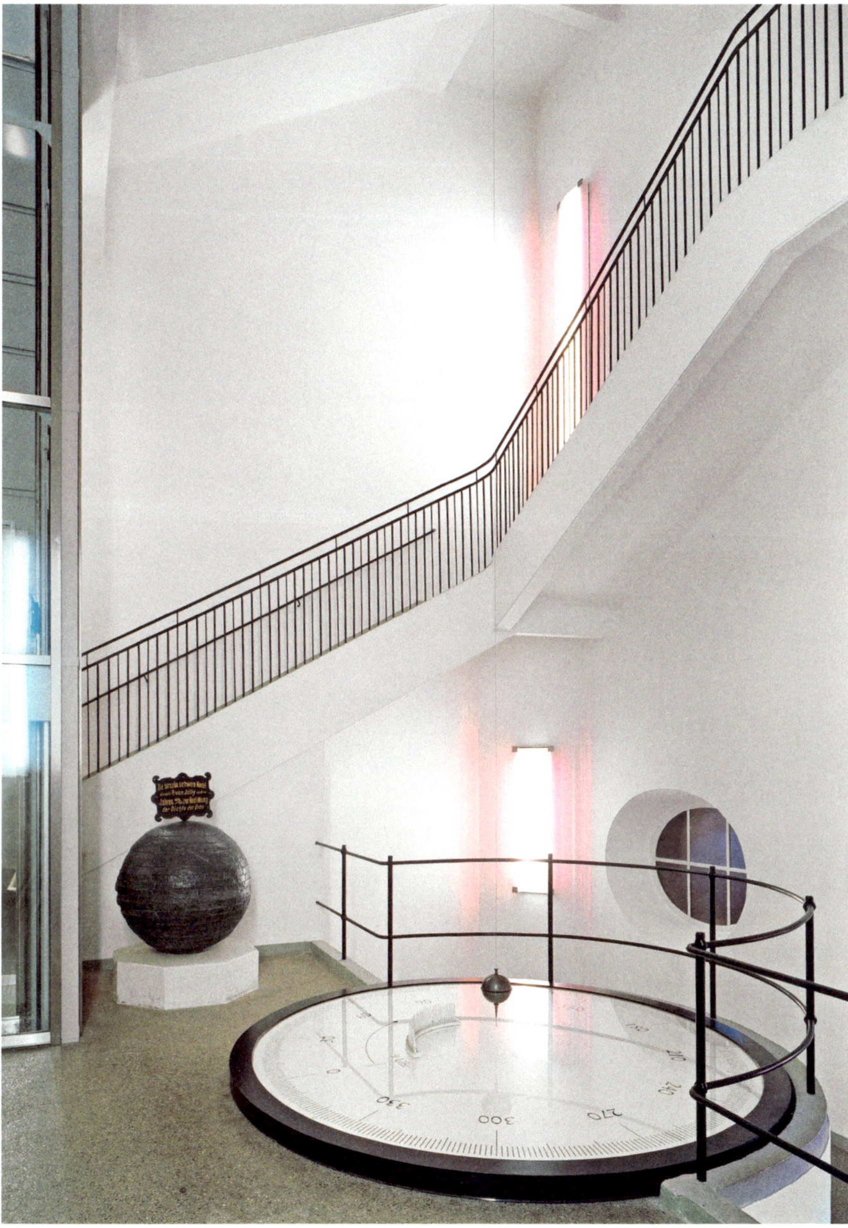

FIG. 2

Foucault's pendulum
in the Deutsches Museum, Munich

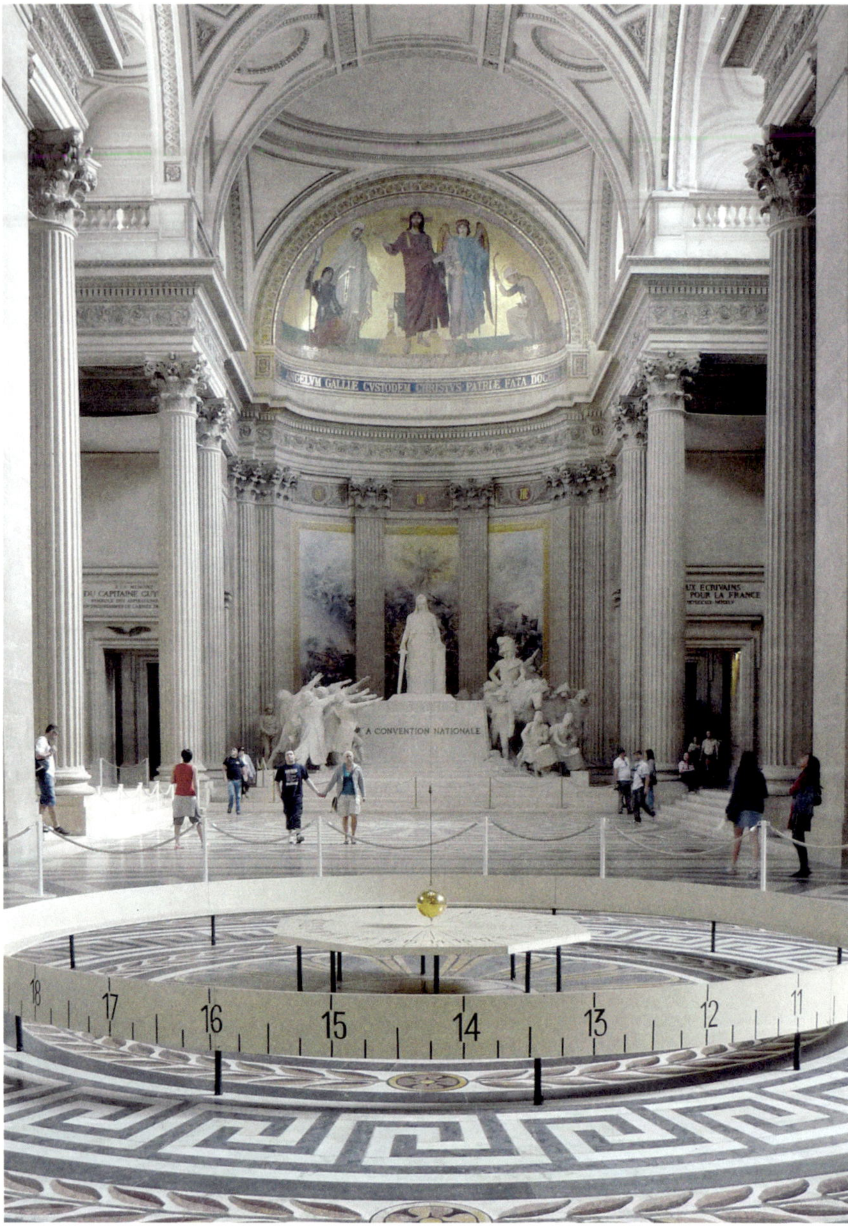

FIG. 3

Foucault's pendulum
in the Panthéon, Paris

A Pendulum for Münster

"When Gerhard Richter presented his plans for an art installation in the deconsecrated Dominican Church in Münster, he revealed that he had already had an idea along these lines in the back of his mind for around ten years."[2] At least that is what a church newspaper reported in late 2017. In fact Richter had already been fascinated by the phenomenon of a Foucault pendulum for over twenty years – the first one he ever saw was in the Deutsches Museum in Munich. This type of pendulum is scientific instrument. It illustrates the observation by French physicist Léon Foucault that the floor beneath a freely swinging pendulum appears to slowly rotate away from it. After an initial experiment at the Paris Observatory, Foucault presented the experiment to the public in 1851 with a pendulum in the dome of the Panthéon suspended on a 67-metre long wire. The plane of oscillation, as physicist Roland Szostak has explained, remains "unchanged in relation to the fixed stars. Therefore, if the Earth rotates under the

---

2 "Gerhard Richter installiert Pendel in Münsters Dominikanerkirche" (see note 1).

pendulum – which it does – then the plane of oscillation rotates relative to the ground that we are standing on. This in itself proves that the Earth is rotating."[3] Foucault's visual demonstration of this fact using a pendulum was the first ever physical proof of the rotation of the Earth (which had already been accepted for centuries by then) and, hence, of the validity of a heliocentric world view.

Following that first encounter with a Foucault pendulum, when Richter was on a trip to Paris he visited the Panthéon where a copy of the original version of the pendulum is still in operation under the dome. Richter then discussed the idea of a pendulum with the Regensburg physicist Franz Giessibl, whose images of atoms (obtained using an atomic force microscope) had previously aroused his interest. In 2013 Richter's preoccupation with the pendulum even led him to construct a model of his own by suspending a steel sphere (already in the inventory of his studio – of which, more later) from the roof of his workshop. To his delight he saw that this makeshift pendulum worked as he had hoped and that the Earth's rotation could be demonstrated by means of strips of paper laid on the floor. Richter also built a table-top model of a pendulum, which he set up in his office, because he now very much hoped one day to install a full-size pendulum somewhere.

Kasper König, who had initiated the series of major sculpture projects in Münster in 1977, saw that model in

---

3 Roland Szostak, "Das Foucault'sche Pendel: Geschichte und Funktion", in *Gerhard Richter: Zwei graue Doppelspiegel für ein Pendel*, Münster [Stadt Münster], [2018], online publication, p. 5.

Richter's studio. In 2017, when König was preparing the fifth exhibition of *Skulptur Projekte Münster*, the city asked him to consider the decommissioned municipal gasometer near the Dortmund-Ems Canal and the city bypass as a

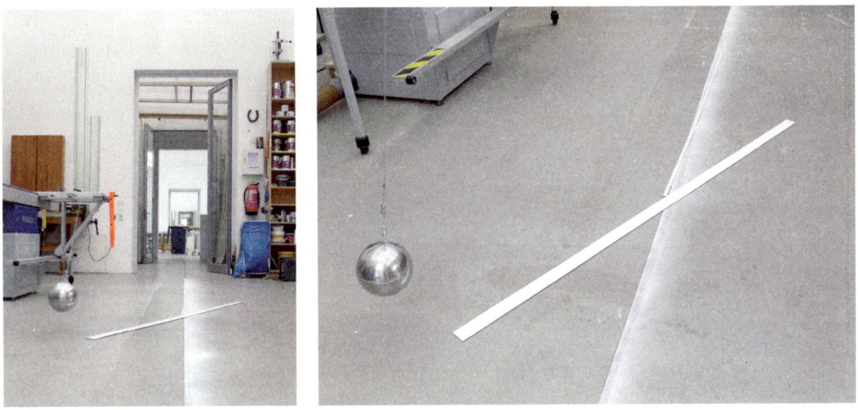

Model of a pendulum in Gerhard Richter's studio, Cologne, 8 August 2013

potential venue, because the council had been trying to identify a cultural use for that area for some time by then. König was not particularly taken by the idea because he felt the gasometer was too spectacular a structure, but then he had the idea of suggesting to Richter that he could use it for his pendulum project, independently of the sculpture exhibition. The volume of the circular structure was impressive: although the tank was only eight metres high, since it was no longer being used to store gas, the open framework around it was 52 metres high with a diameter of

56 metres. On 23 May 2016 König met Gail Kirkpatrick, director of Kunsthalle Münster, who also had responsibility for art in public spaces in Münster, and Marcus Lütkemeyer, who was co-curating an exhibition at the Kunsthalle at the time, and told them about his idea. They liked it, so König called Richter and asked him to create a proposal for this location. Richter, quite elated, replied that same day and sent König a sheaf of sketches. And the very next day he contacted Giessibl with some practical questions regarding the realization of a pendulum. Since the top of the gasometer was open and had no suitable suspension point for a pendulum, Richter had come up with a construction that could be used instead; he also created drawings for oscillations of four, twelve, and twenty metres.

After that Kirkpatrick took the initiative with help from Lütkemeyer and gained support from Cornelia Wilkens, the head of cultural affairs on the city council. Richter was duly invited to visit Münster and on 7 July 2016 he, Kirkpatrick and Wilkens went to inspect the gasometer. As it turned out, the sight of that monument to industry on the outskirts of Münster came as something of a disappointment to Richter – it was spray-painted inside and out with graffiti and clearly the pendulum would continually be exposed to the weather. However, before Richter left the city again, Wilkens raised the possibility of the Dominican Church in the city centre as an alternative. No sooner said than done, they went to see it and Richter was immediately drawn to the church, which is surrounded on all sides by faceless offices and commercial properties. "You could see that Richter liked it," remembers Wilkens, "and then he said he could imagine more than just a pendulum there."[4] Kirkpatrick also recalled that moment: "When we walked into the church Gerhard Richter was immediately struck by its monumental dimensions, by the atmosphere and the elegance of its well proportioned spaces, which almost mirror each other. The longitudinal alignment of this sacred structure is balanced by the very secular notion of a central space in a manner that is calming, moving, and inspiring. We had found the right place for the pendulum."[5]

That impression is confirmed in a letter that Richter sent to Münster on 11 July: "This church interior would not only give the necessary protection, it would also provide a suitable setting that – with its architectural excellence and its historical associations – would communicate a very welcome seriousness."[6] In the following weeks Kirkpatrick and Richter discussed various issues by telephone. The church was still being used for worship by the Catholic community at the Westfälische Wilhelms-Universität Münster (WWU Münster). There was a round altar table under the crossed dome and an organ on the west wall, both of which were still in use. The organ was in fact a later addition to the church; as well as that, in the nave

---

4 "Gerhard Richter will Münster ein 'Foucaultsches Pendel' schenken", *Münstersche Zeitung*, 22 September 2017, online report.

5 *Gerhard Richter: Zwei graue Doppelspiegel für ein Pendel* (see note 3), p. 2.

6 Gerhard Richter to Gail Kirkpatrick, email on 16 July 2016 (Gerhard Richter Archive).

there was a model of the city of Münster on a scale of 1:500. Although another visit by Richter, scheduled for 23 August, had to be cancelled, Kirkpatrick kept the project moving and made contact with the Department of Physics at the WWU Münster, in order to discuss the technicalities of installing a pendulum. In November 2016 confirmation came that it was possible to install a pendulum of that kind in the church, and the news was immediately conveyed to Gerhard Richter. On 31 March 2017 Wilkens, Kirkpatrick, and Lütkemeyer visited Richter in his studio in Cologne and discussed the future of the project in detail. It was on this occasion that Richter first put forward his idea of a larger work of art as such, not just a pendulum; he also explained that this would be a gift from him to the city of Münster. Once experts had examined the structural aspects of the plan, a project group was set up in April, with representatives from various municipal offices. Hubert Becker, from Gerhard Richter's studio, co-ordinated the process.

In mid-June 2017 Richter presented his plan for a pendulum with two pairs of grey mirrors, one on either side.[7] A month later, when he visited the exhibition *Skulptur Projekte Münster*, he also went to see the church again, specifically to check his vision against the reality of the situation and to discuss it with various city office holders, including Mayor Markus Lewe. Discussions were held regarding the circumstances of the installation, above all

---

7 Gerhard Richter to Gail Kirkpatrick, email on 12 June 2017 (Gerhard Richter Archive).

how visitor access would be regulated. It was also agreed that in future no other works of art would be shown in the church either temporarily or permanently and that any other use of the space should respect the requirements of the installation. Furthermore, the model of the city would be removed from the church. On 1 September another meeting was held at Richter's studio; physicist Prof. Dr. Roland Szostak was present in order to discuss in detail the design and realization of the pendulum. Richter had prepared a list of technical questions for that meeting, some of which reflected his concern regarding the autonomous functioning of the pendulum: "By how many degrees does the amplitude axis shift per hour and in which direction? Clockwise? How long does it take for the pendulum to return to its starting point? Can the axis displacement of the pendulum be calculated in advance so that the axis position can be given at a certain time, e.g., after five years? If the operation of the pendulum has to be re-started after an interruption, can a 'correct' starting point be defined? Would there be a 'correct' starting point for the pendulum when it is first taken into operation?"[8]

While Richter was engaged in his own artistic deliberations, the city of Münster grappled with creating the conditions needed for a work of art to be installed in the Dominican Church. The politicians discussed the proposal by the city's head of cultural affairs to re-dedicate

---

8 Gerhard Richter, undated note (Gerhard Richter Archive).

the church to art and how to manage the change-of-use and the necessary renovations. At the council meeting on 18 October 2017 the draft resolution was unanimously passed and the council duly took note that the artist proposed to gift the work to the city of Münster, which "would only have to bear the production and installation costs." Of the estimated total cost of 650,000 Euros for production and installation, 600,000 had already been promised in donations from the state of North Rhine-Westphalia, the Stiftung der Sparkasse Münsterland Ost, the Verein der Kaufmannschaft zu Münster, and the Freundeskreis der Kunsthalle Münster, which meant that the city only had to find the remaining 50,000 Euros. In return the city undertook to secure the work's future and to make it permanently accessible to the public. Gerhard Richter was very happy when news of this reached him the following day.

On 12 November 2017 the church was deconsecrated by Auxiliary Bishop Stefan Zekorn, and the university's Catholic community relocated, if rather reluctantly, to another church, St. Ludgeri. Just a few weeks later, on 30 November, Gerhard Richter – together with Cornelia Wilkens and Mayor Markus Lewe – presented the finalized project in the church. As to the execution of the installation, Richter sent a note to Kirkpatrick: "I can only take care of the two wall objects and advise on aesthetic issues regarding the pendulum. That's as much as I can do."[9]

---

9 Marginal note on an email from Gail Kirkpatrick dated 23 November 2017.

Work began on the installation in the New Year and was completed, on time, in May 2018.

After the inauguration of the work in June 2018 the question was raised as to whether the high altar with the Stations of the Cross could remain in the church. Richter was in favour and suggested that the choir screen be retained and that the high altar be left where it was in the choir. The only change he proposed was that the gate in the choir screen be replaced with a neutral door, so that the areas occupied by the pendulum and the choir respectively would be quite separate. That suggestion was implemented during additional building work in 2019–20.

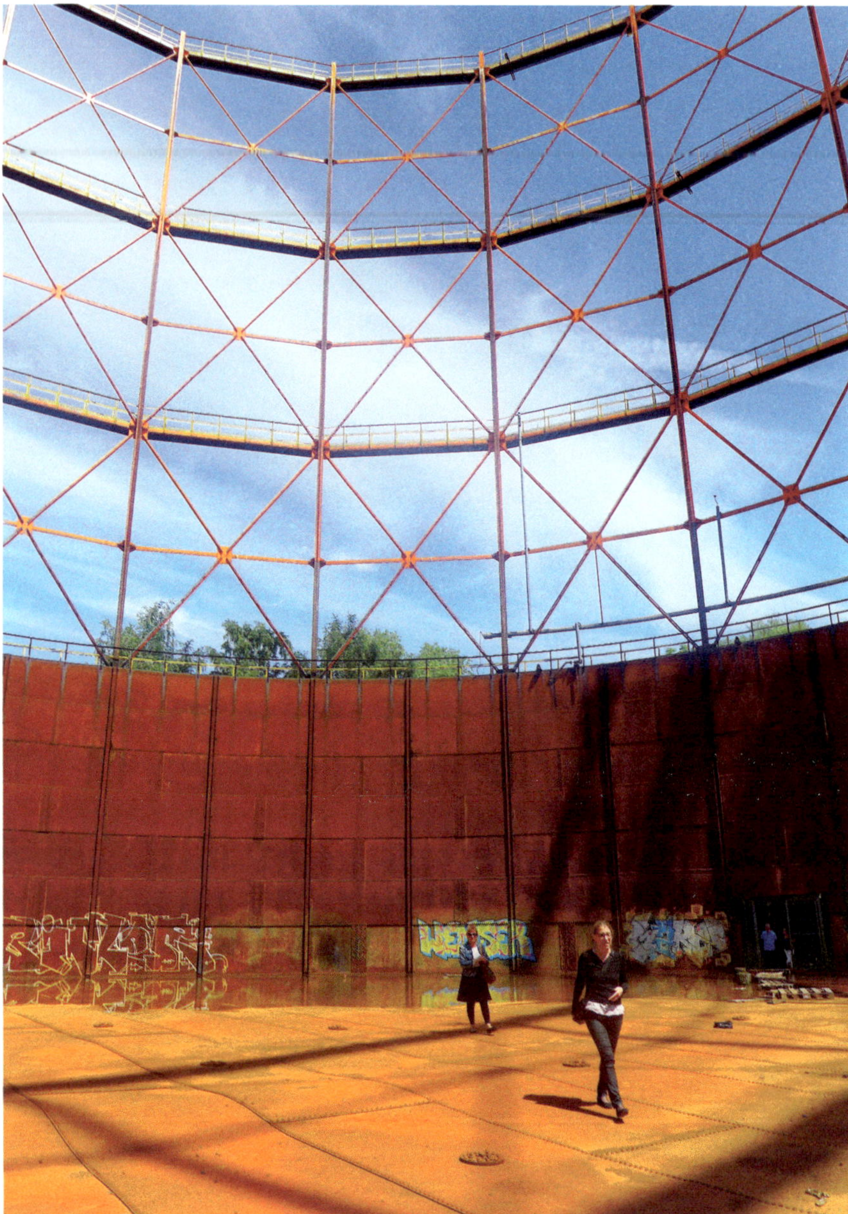

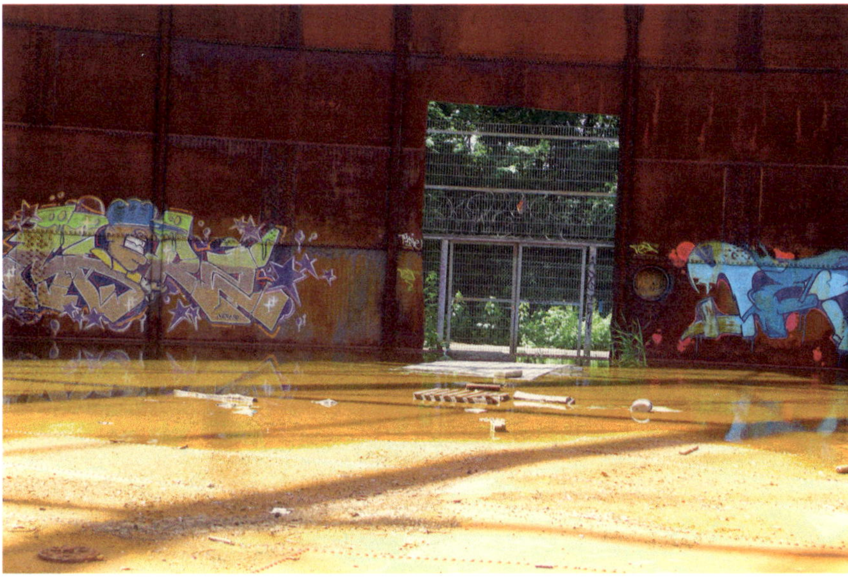

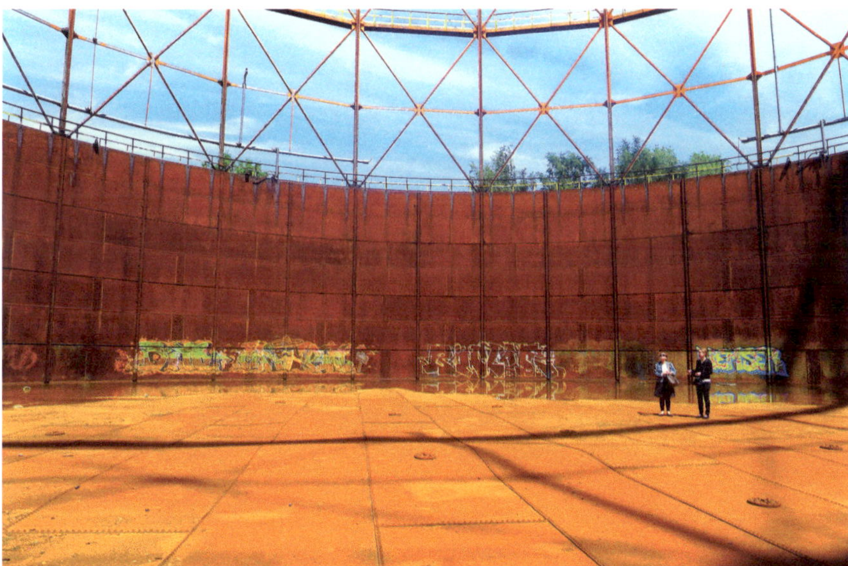

FIGS. 4–6

Exploratory visit to the gasometer in Münster,
7 July 2016

22.5.11

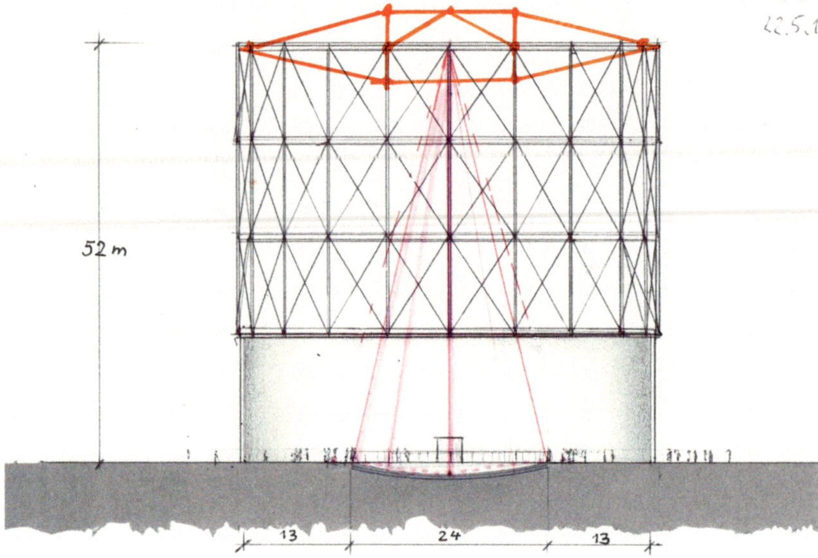

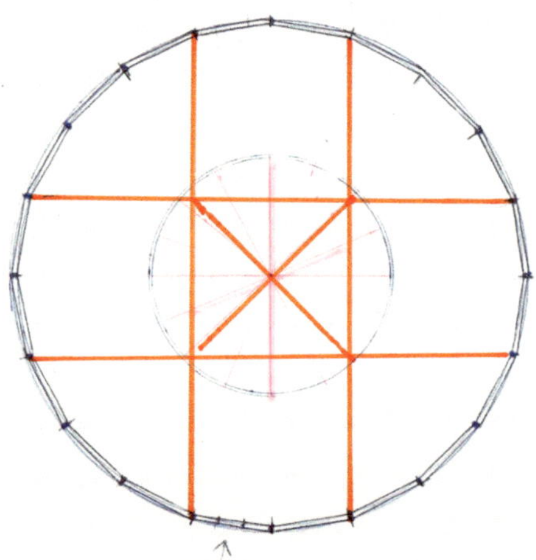

1 : 500

Foucault - Pendel ca. 50 m

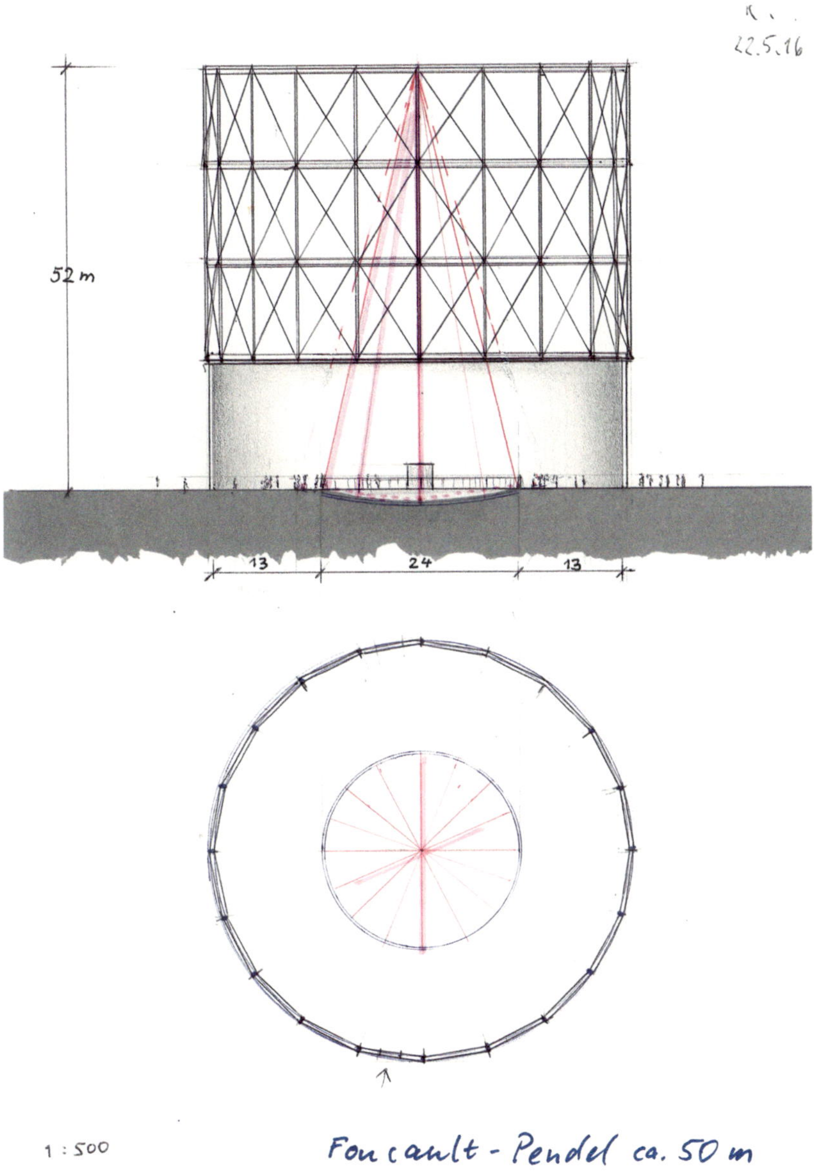

FIGS. 7 and 8

Drawings illustrating the suspension of a Foucault's pendulum and the design of the plane of oscillation in the gasometer in Münster, 22 May 2016

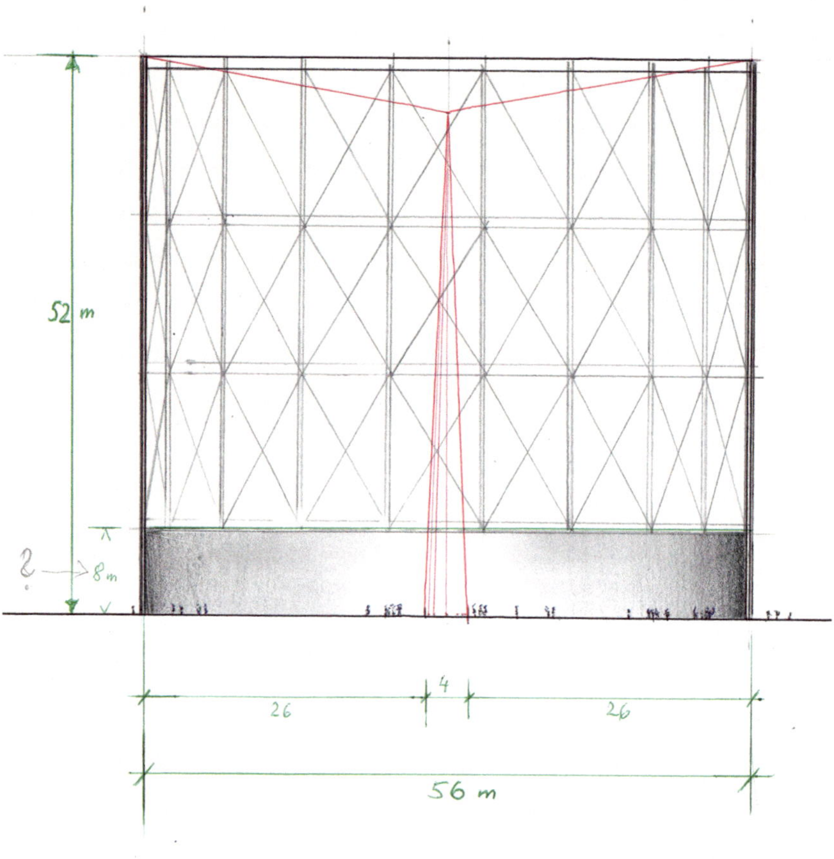

52 m
8 m
4
26
26
56 m

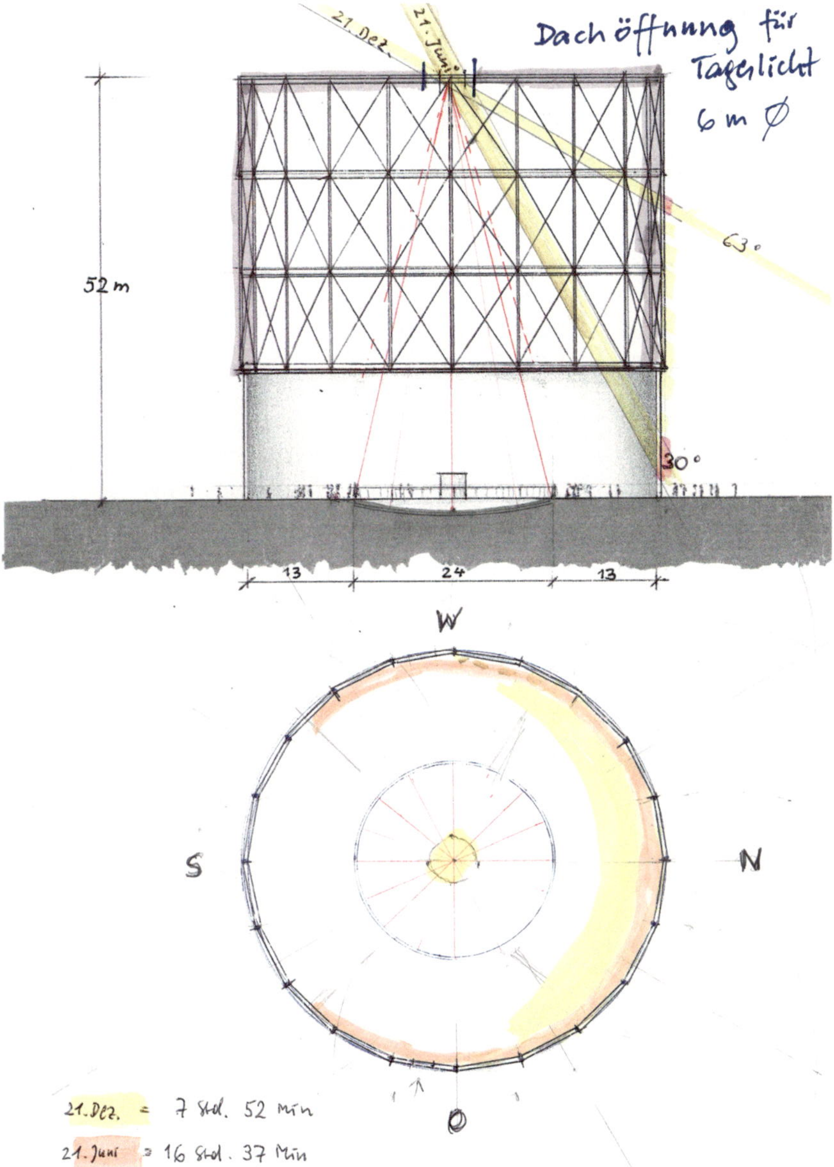

FIGS. 9 and 10

Drawings illustrating the suspension of a Foucault's pendulum and the design of the plane of oscillation in the gasometer in Münster, 22 May 2016

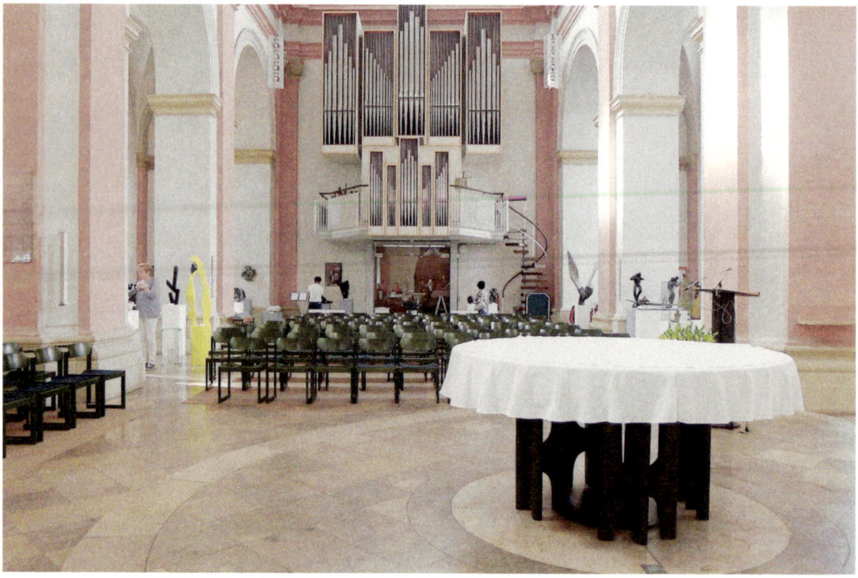

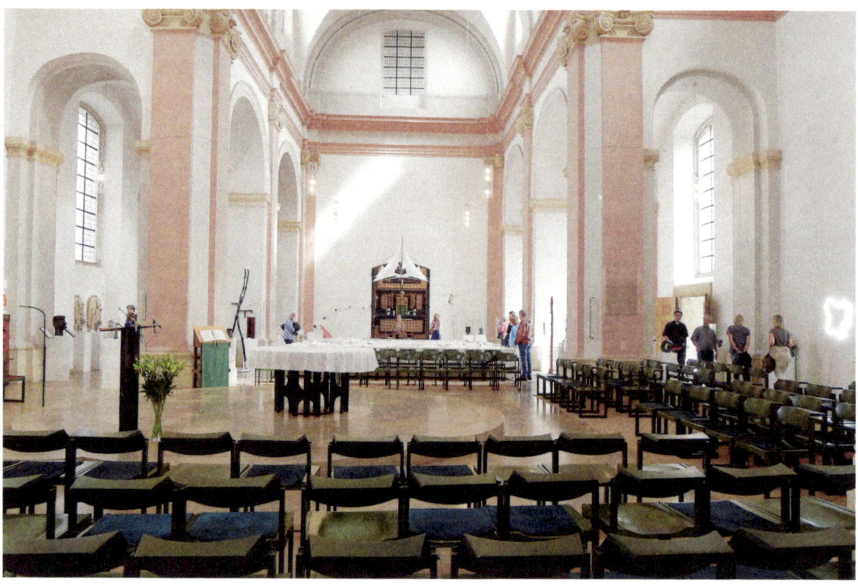

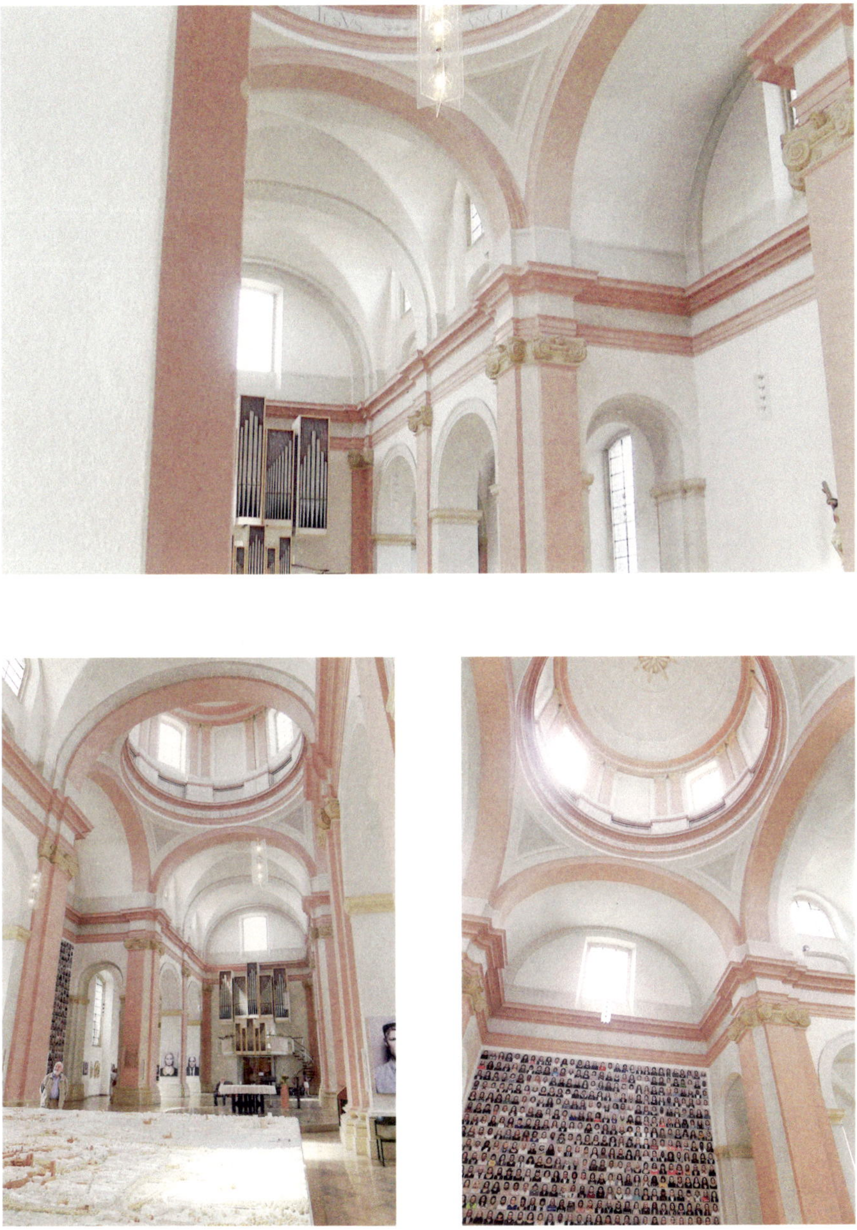

FIGS. 11–15

Interior of the Dominikanerkirche, Münster, as it was on 7 July 2016

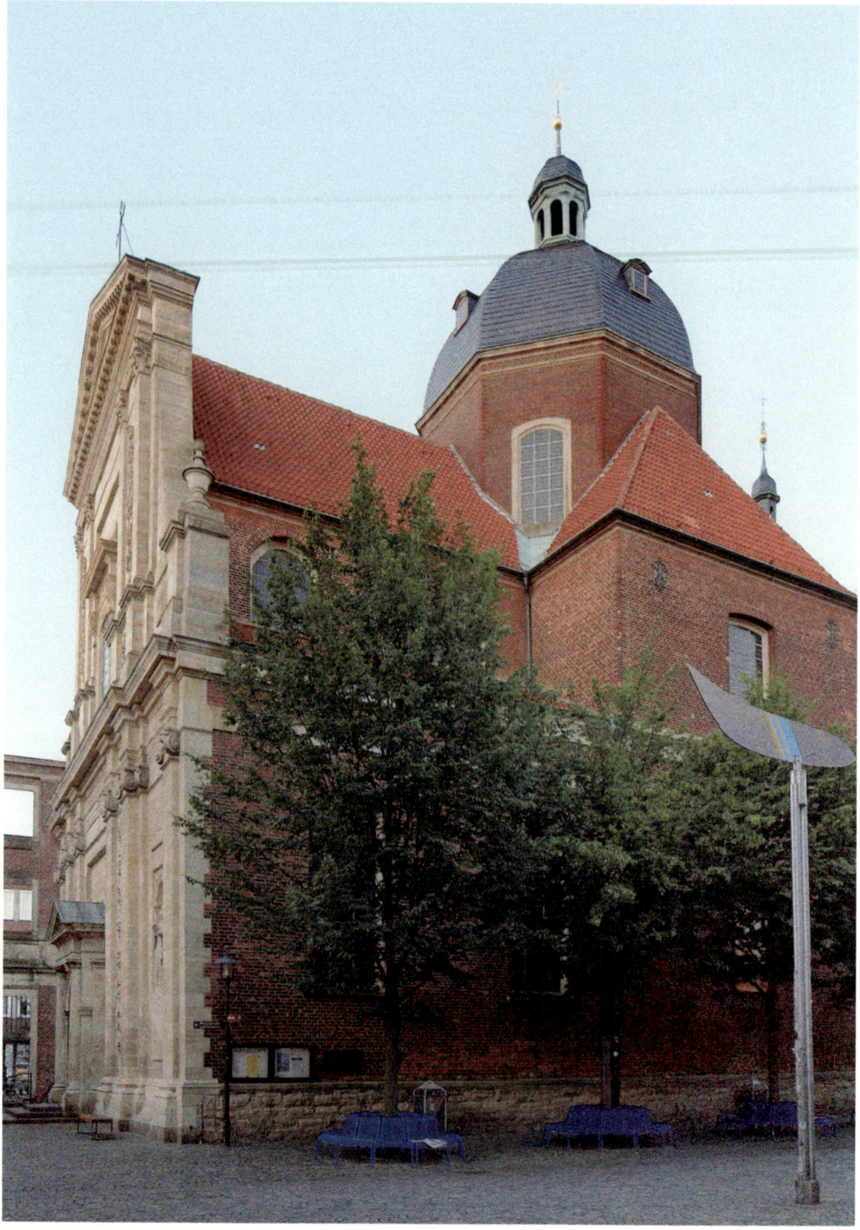

FIG. 16

Exterior of the Dominikanerkirche
in Münster

The Place and the Work

The Dominican Church was part of a monastery complex that was built for the Dominicans between 1708 and 1725; members of the order had moved from Osnabrück to Münster in the fourteenth century. The drawings for the church were done by Lambert Friedrich Corfey, an architect based in Münster, who had studied important examples of French and Italian Baroque architecture on an extended trip through France and Italy. Thus the sandstone basilica in Münster, with its central lantern dome around thirty-four metres above ground, is reminiscent of already somewhat classical, French Baroque architecture. The church was consecrated in 1728; in 1811 Napoleon dissolved the monastery, and the buildings were subsequently used as a "military assembly depot" where cannons and howitzers were repaired. After the city of Münster acquired the church in 1881, it was used as the school church for the municipal secondary school. Towards the end of World War II the church was very severely damaged during an air raid; in 1960 it was reconstructed by the state of North Rhine-Westphalia. All that is left of the monastery, however, is the facade of the entrance. It was during that reconstruction that the altar table was placed under the crossed dome and the choir screen was reinstated, separating the choir with its Baroque high altar from the nave.

As to the interior of the church, with its white sandstone walls framed by pink horizontals and verticals, Marlies Voss, head of the city's Department of Historic Monuments, has described it as a "three-naved, groin-vaulted basilica with a central dome and lantern, with narrow, transept-like side spaces. As the church for a mendicant order the architecture has a striking simplicity and almost no ornamentation. The magnificent proportions of its spatial composition thus appear all the more impressive."[10] The cool elegance of this space looked to Richter like the ideal setting for the permanent installation of a work of art.

For Richter, this situation was particularly appealing because a pendulum suspended from the central dome would be in almost the same position as Foucault's pendulum in the Panthéon. Although the church has no transept, the crossing in the centre of the nave – and hence the openings towards the side walls – is emphasised by the free-standing crossing piers. In the months after Richter's visit to Münster, he further refined his ideas; he decided to add a specially designed base plate and two pairs of vertical glass paintings on the side walls. Thus the work was no longer solely about putting a pendulum in place; it was now about a composition with a wider range that would connect the pendulum and the space, reflecting the new

---

10 Marlies Voss, "Die Dominikanerkirche: Geschichte und Gebäude", in *Gerhard Richter: Zwei graue Doppelspiegel für ein Pendel* (see note 3), p. 7.

circumstances. As he always does for exhibitions and construction projects, Richter made a model in his studio on a scale of 1:50, consisting of a side wall, the pendulum, and human figures as a way of familiarizing himself with the situation, playing around with ideas, and taking the necessary decisions.

Otten, consulting civil engineers in Münster, conducted the calculations for the suspension of the pendulum and initially proposed creating a tubular steel structure inside the dome. However, following the site visit on 30 November 2017, when Otten reviewed the situation, it proved possible to do without any such addition, which Richter had found rather conspicuous. The engineers were now able to demonstrate that the dome had sufficient load-bearing capacity for the pendulum. This also allowed the length of the pendulum wire to be increased from 20 to 29 metres. Although this greater length is not obvious from the movement of the pendulum, the viewer looking upwards would now see that the pendulum extends the full vertical height of the dome.

On Richter's request, Giessibl designed a prototype pendulum "bob", as the sphere suspended from the wire is called. The final version of the bob was produced by the local precision-engineering company NBF Norbert Bücker; it is a non-magnetic metal sphere with a diameter of 22 cm, which is suspended on a 28.75-metre steel wire. The bob has a brass core, which is gold-plated and silver-passivated, giving it the appearance of a stainless steel ball. Its weight of 48 kg is needed to ensure a steady swing. Directly below the suspension point there is a Charron ring, with a diameter of 7 cm, which neutralises any external forces

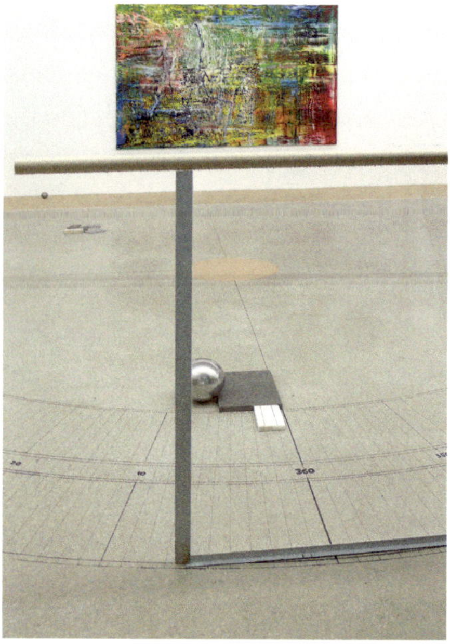

Model of the plane of oscillation in Gerhard Richter's studio, Cologne, 18 January 2018

that could disturb the steady motion of the pendulum. In order to ensure that the pendulum does not come to a standstill due to frictional losses, an electromagnetic pendulum drive is housed below the centre of the plane of oscillation; this drive was designed and constructed by the Physics Department workshop at the WWU Münster. A magnet attached to the bob receives a pulse from a magnetic coil, which ensures that it continues to oscillate evenly.

Richter's initial plans, drawn up in 2017, already provided for a pendulum with an inner and outer oscillation range of 4 and 5.6 metres respectively; these measurements would not change. Richter then paid special attention to that zone because the only visible evidence of the Earth's rotation is derived from the markings on the base plate. During the site visit in July 2017 Richter declared that he wanted to create a special finish for the floor beneath the pendulum. Initially he toyed with the idea of a slight hollow. Then at the meeting in Cologne on 1 September the idea of a plane – with incised markings – set into the floor of the church was aired. Subsequently Richter drew the circle divided into degrees full-size on the studio floor, so that he could pace it out and check its dimensions and the thickness of the dividing lines. Bearing in mind the situation at the Panthéon, he also experimented with the idea of a safety rail enclosing the pendulum's plane of oscillation.[11]

Ultimately the area beneath the plane of oscillation was not just marked on the floor of the church; it was embodied in a circular slab of stone. Once again the design process went through a number of stages; having at first considered using greywacke for the centre and beige marble for the outer ring, Richter finally decided to use only greywacke for the whole piece.[12] Greywacke is a sandstone and it is related to the stone used for the Dominican Church,

---

11 A safety rail or barrier of that kind is included in certain models, see figs. 19–23, and visible in certain drawings, see figs. 26–28.

12 On the drawing dated 7 February 2018 the base plate was to be made from a greywacke centre and an outer ring of marble.

although it is a darker grey because of its lower quartz content. It is generally found in Paleozoic strata, that is to say, it is extremely ancient and, as such, creates an air of permanence that is well-suited to the ongoing motion of the pendulum. The central area of the stone is concave, matching the swing of the pendulum just four centimetres above it. This area has been impregnated, making it appear darker, while the outer circle retains its original paler grey. On the drawings done in November 2017 the inner zone is divided into 24 segments of 15° each, while the outer ring is divided into 12 segments of 30° each. However, Richter changed this in the final version: the inner zone is now divided into 12 segments of 30°, while the outer ring – with much smaller divisions – is (in a break with tradition) divided into 10 segments of 36°, which of course do not line up with the markings in the inner zone. The starting point of the division into degrees lies on the west-facing longitudinal axis of the building. Ideally the plane of oscillation would complete a full rotation during the course of 24 hours, like Planet Earth. However, that only occurs at the north or the south pole; everywhere else on Earth the full rotation takes longer. In Münster it takes around 30 hours, which means that during the course of one hour a clockwise rotation of around 12° can be observed.

Although this ensemble is placed in the centre of the building, it does not dominate the space because the steel wire is so fine that it is not immediately visible; the bob is low down – at the lower edge of one's field of vision – and the grey stone slab only stands minimally proud of the floor. And the viewer does not discover the two pairs of mirrors, which are also part of the ensemble, until he or she approaches the pendulum and enters the crossing with its open views towards the north and south walls. However, it is not possible to overlook the mirrors because there are no deep side aisles and the double mirrors are hung on walls that are close to the viewer and framed by a pilaster on either side. The steel braces used to mount the mirrors on the walls are hidden from sight, so that the glass seems to be floating. Richter took his time over deciding on the exact dimensions of these tall mirrors. Initially he considered a format of 600 × 200 cm, but then he reduced the width to 134 cm, giving the mirrors a more slender look. One undated sketch has a green-blue pair of mirrors on one wall and three, evenly grey mirrors on the opposite wall – with each set arranged symmetrically.[13] In November 2017, besides a green-blue pair Richter also considered a red-yellow pair, and at one point he even experimented with sets of four coloured mirrors, since he felt at the time that these would work better than the grey mirrors.[14] The two pairs of mirrors, each with two different grey tones – as they appear in the finished work – are first seen in a sketch dated 12 December 2017.[15] It is clear

13 Gerhard Richter, *Atlas*, p. 810 (unpublished), Städtische Galerie im Lenbachhaus, Munich.

14 Gerhard Richter to Gail Kirkpatrick, email on 7 November 2017 (Gerhard Richter Archive).

15 Gerhard Richter, draft plans, 12 December 2017 (Gerhard Richter Archive).

from that drawing that the mirrors are aligned with the oscillation zone and that the width of the top edge of the pairs of mirrors corresponds to the oscillation width of the pendulum at that point. There is thus a direct visual relationship between the different elements of the work. On a drawing done on 7 March 2018 and in drawings of details of the two pairs of mirrors, the grey tones are identified by their official colour numbers.

The panes of glass used in the final version of the work were enamelled grey from behind and the front sides were vaporized with a reflective coating. The panes are mounted side-by-side at a distance of 10 centimetres from the wall, however, they do not form a single continuum because the two panes in each pair are not the same grey hue: the panes on the left side of each pair are an identical dark grey, however, in each case the other pane is slightly paler (to different degrees). This barely perceptible difference and the placing of the different grey tones cuts across the symmetrical order around the crossing without impinging on it.

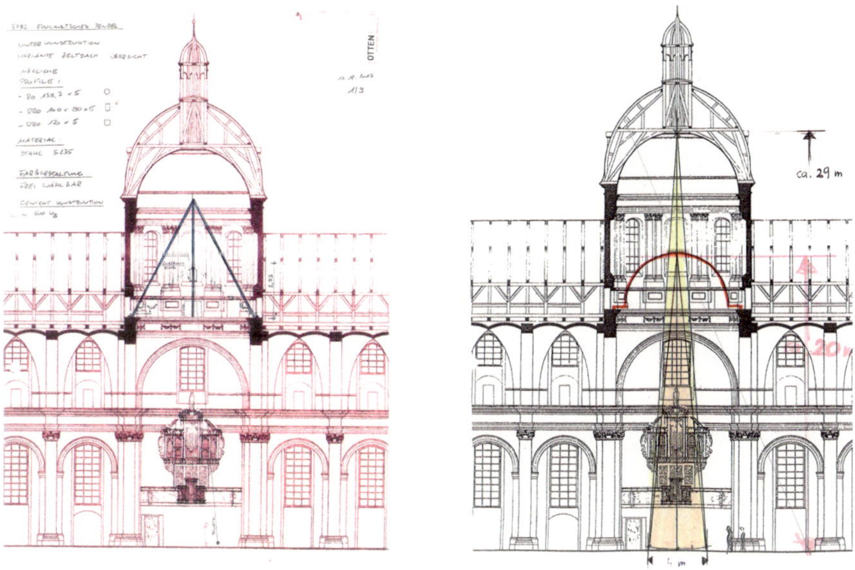

FIGS. 17 and 18

Drawings illustrating the suspension of a pendulum in the Dominikanerkirche, with and without an internal support structure, 13 December 2017

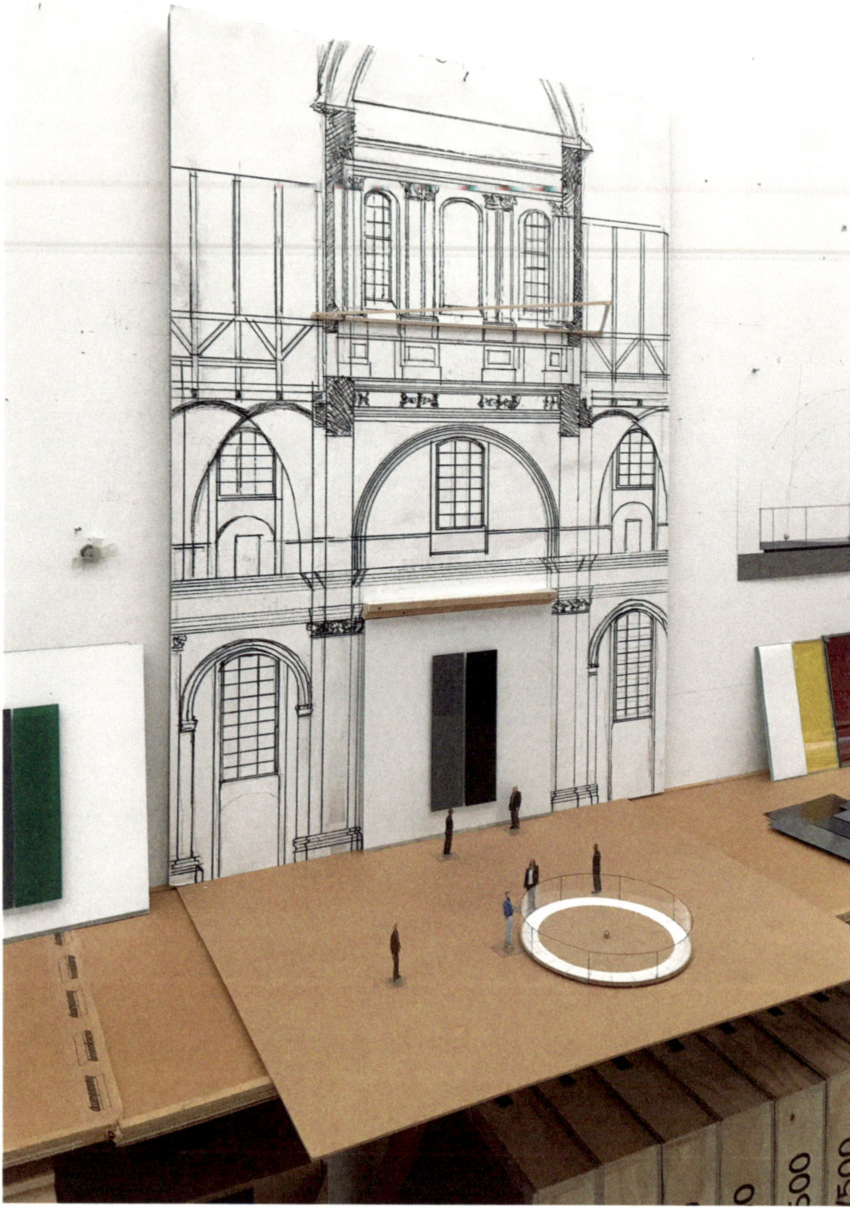

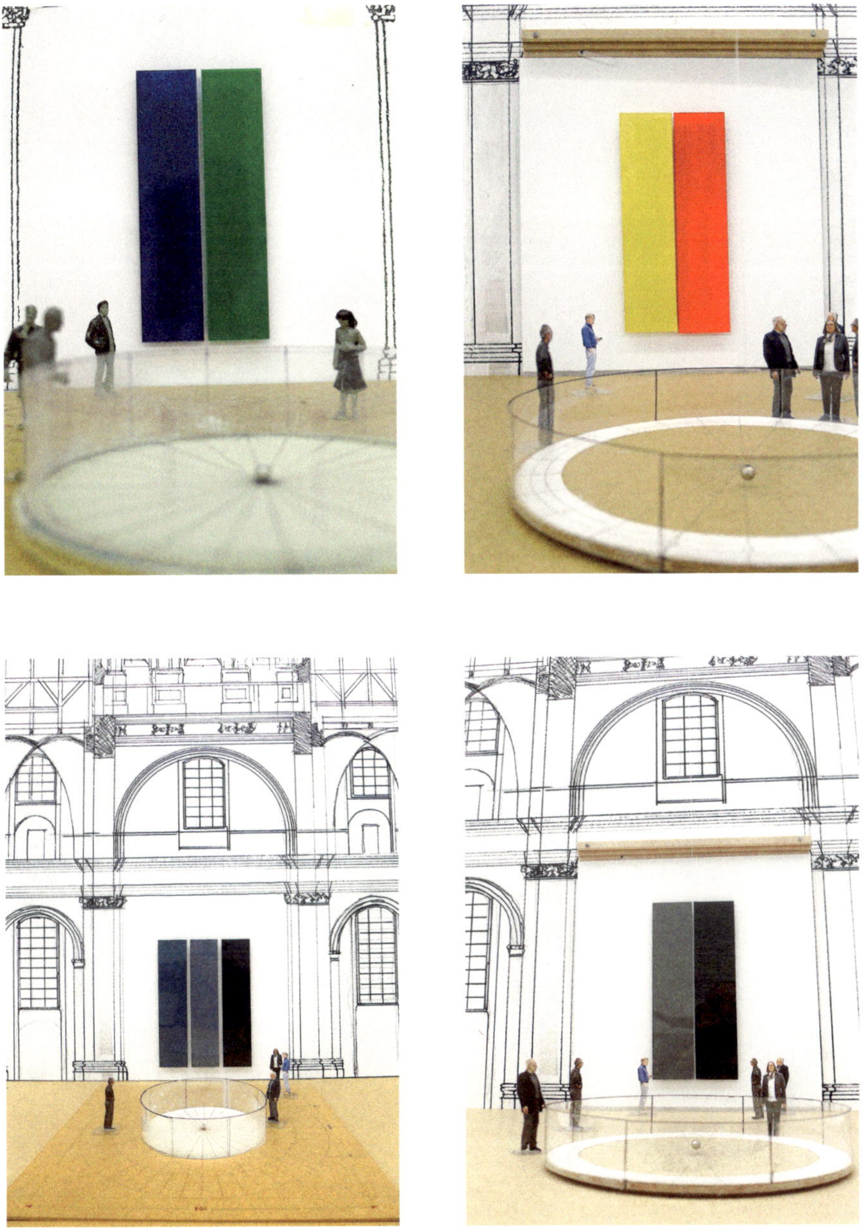

FIGS. 19–23

Model with pendulum and double mirrors
in Gerhard Richter's studio, Cologne, November 2017

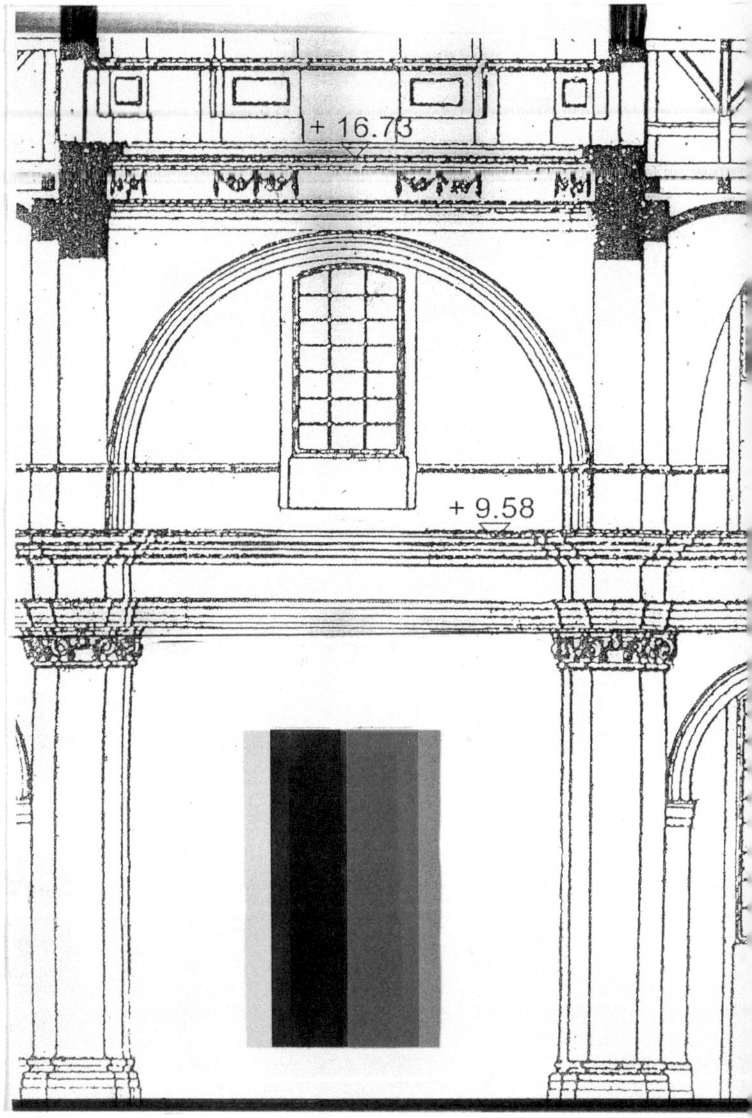
+ 16.73
+ 9.58

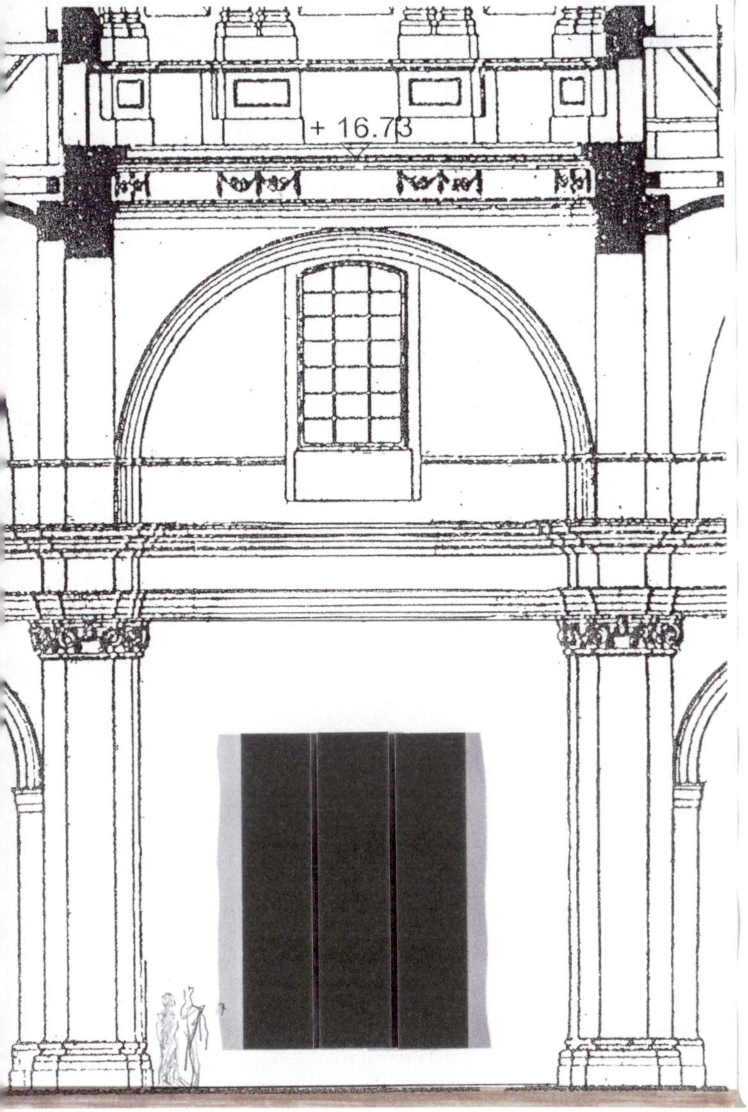

FIG. 24

Atlas, sheet 810, 2017

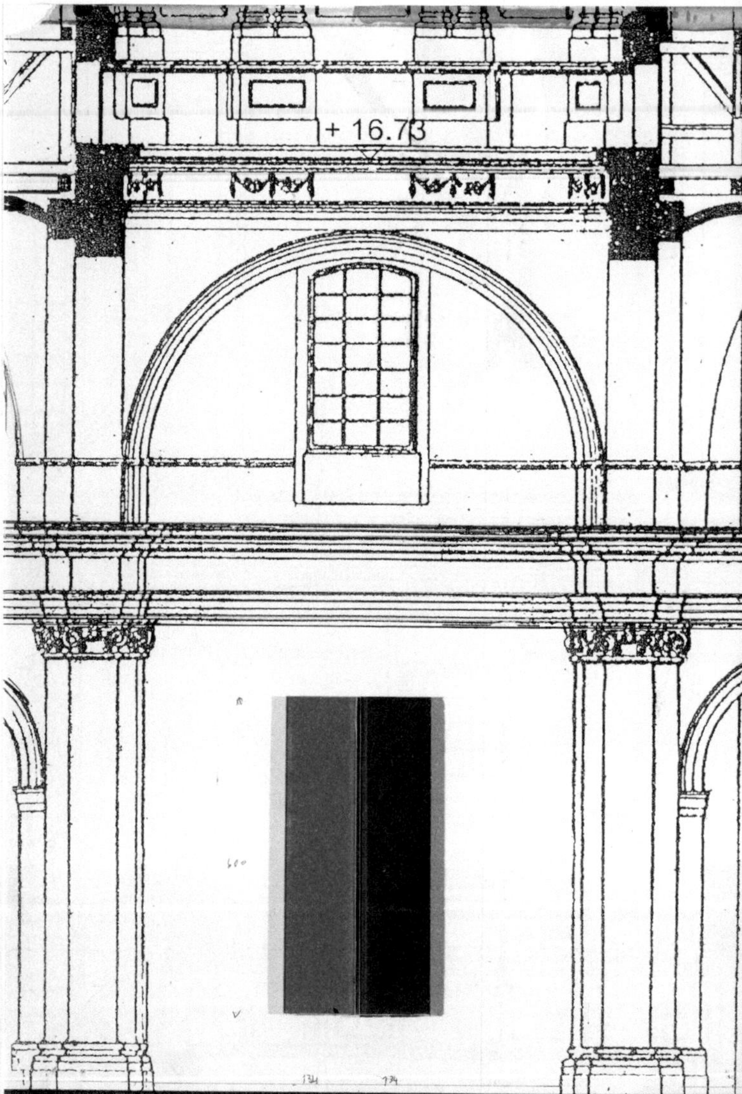
+ 16.73

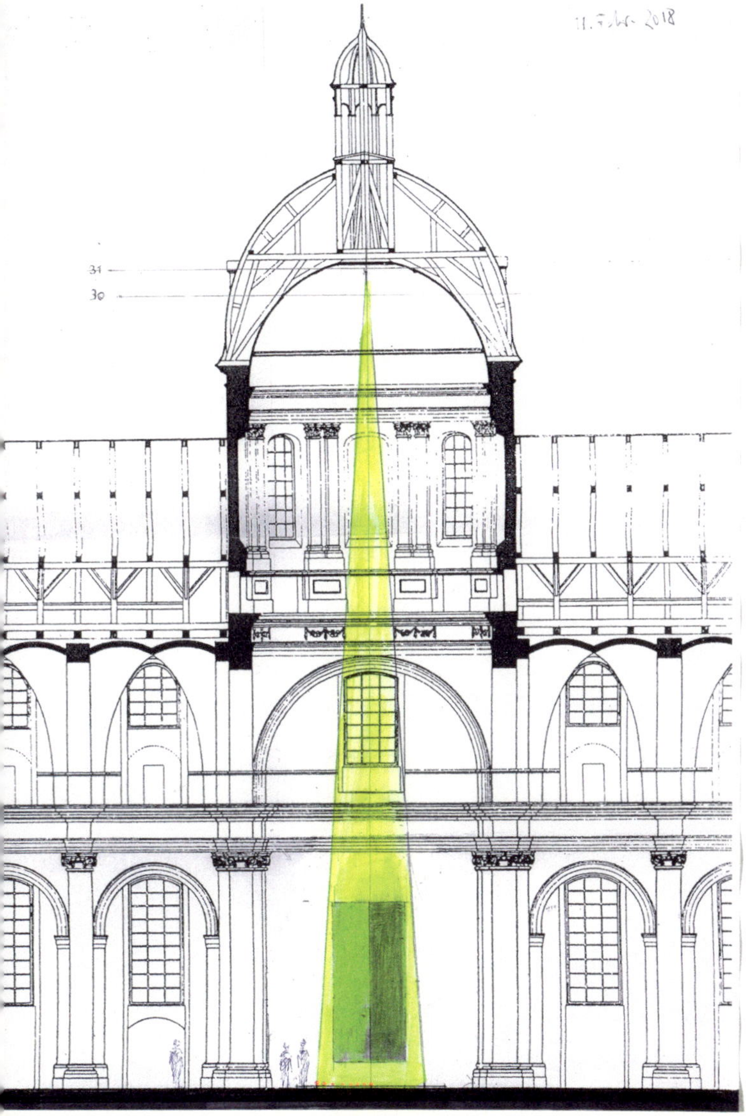

FIG. 25

Atlas, sheet 811, 2017, 2018

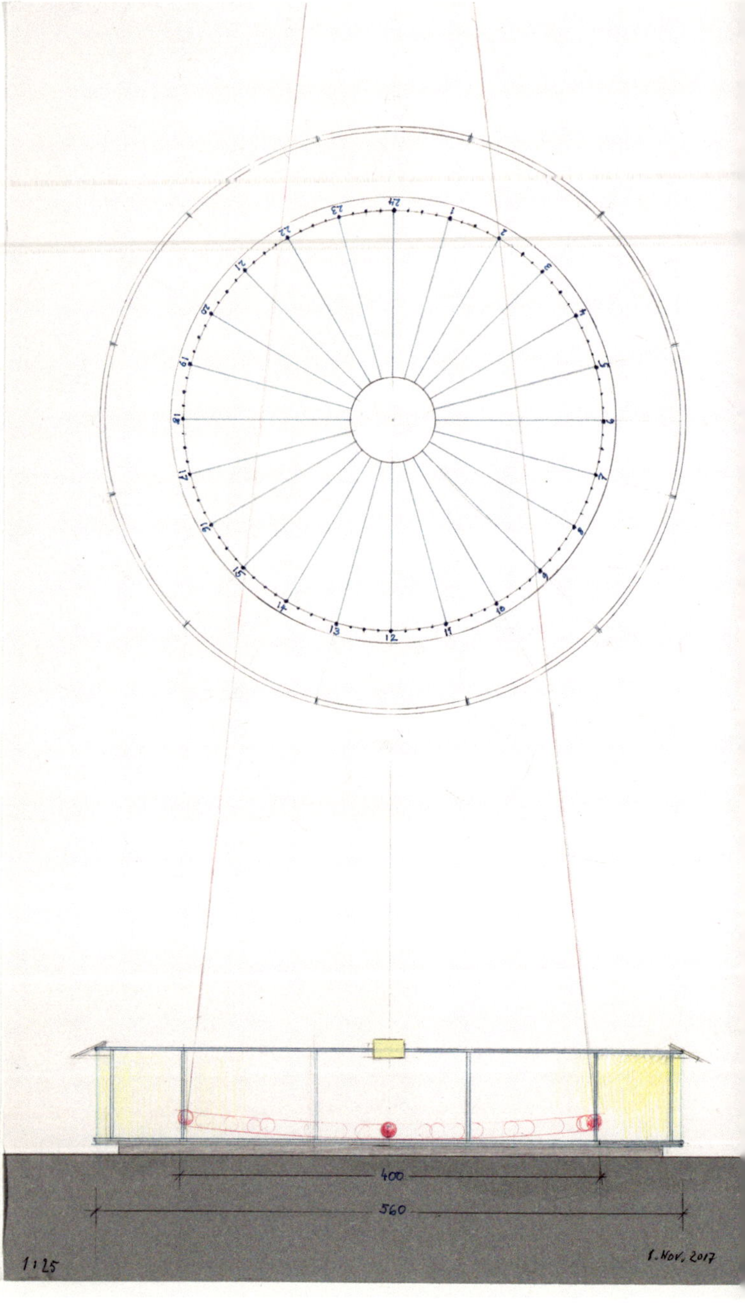
400
560
1:25
1. Nov. 2017

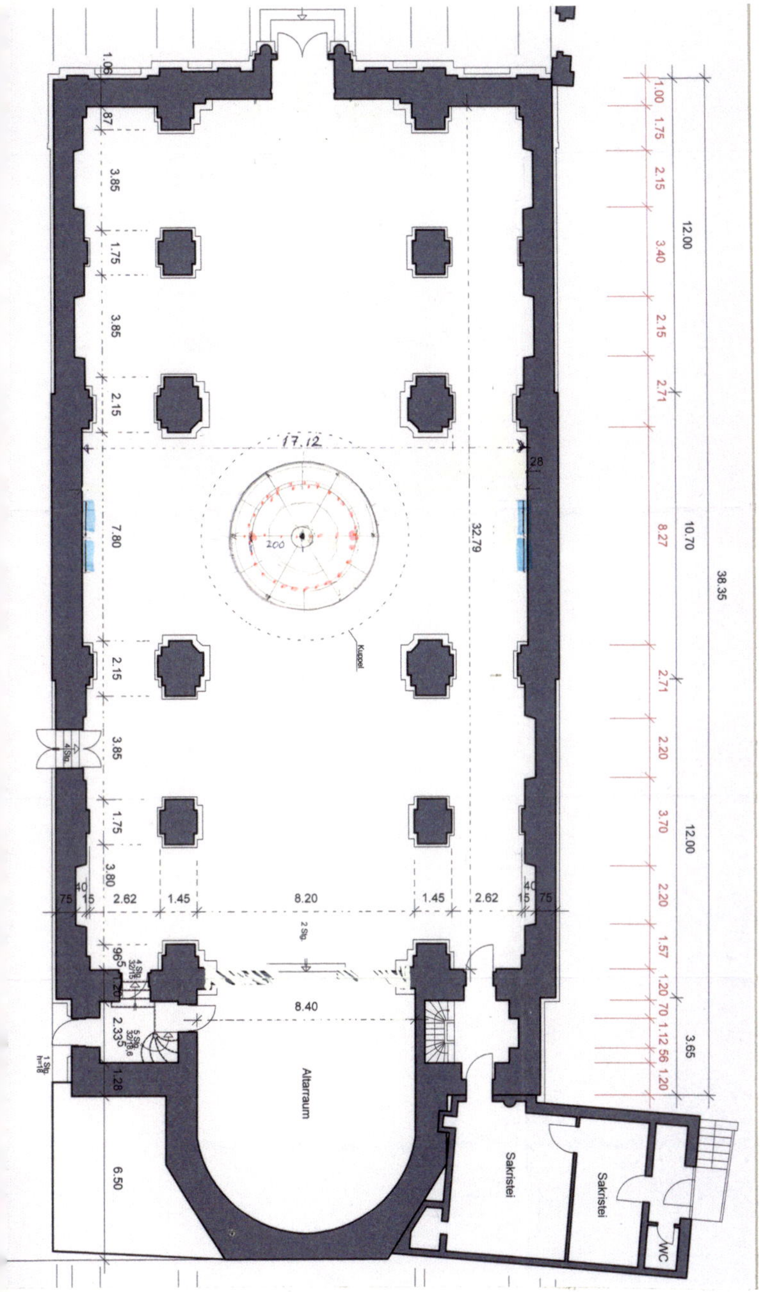

FIG. 26

Atlas, sheet 812, 2017

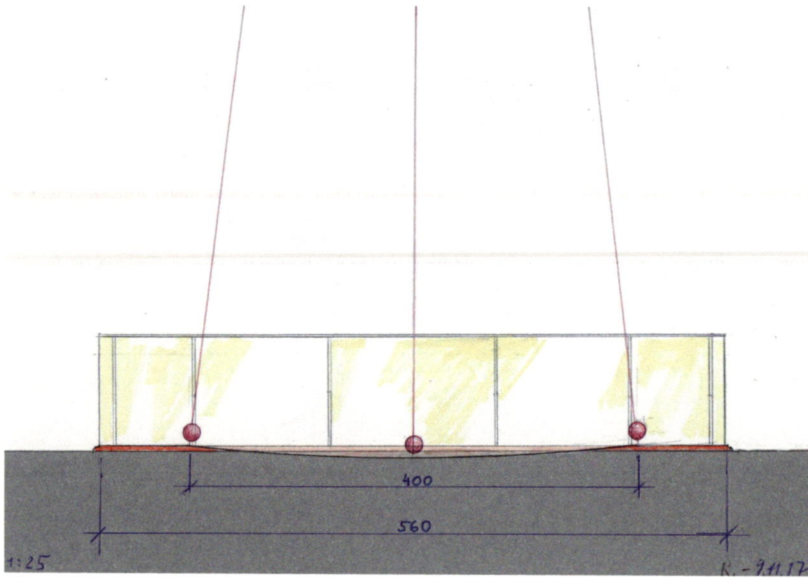

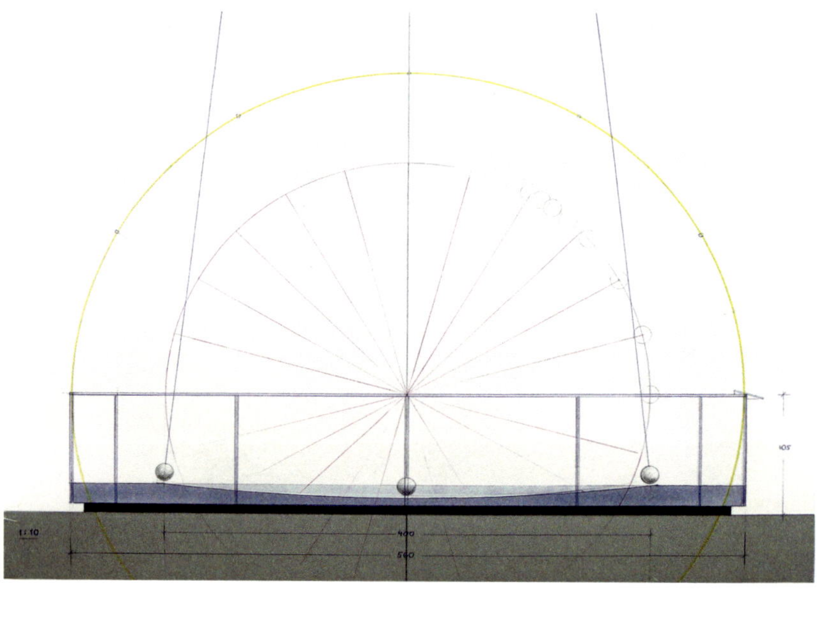

FIGS. 27 and 28

Drawings of the pendulum's plane of oscillation, 9 November 2017

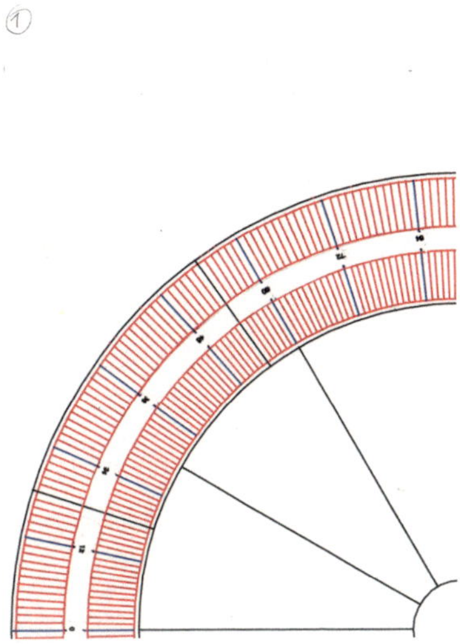

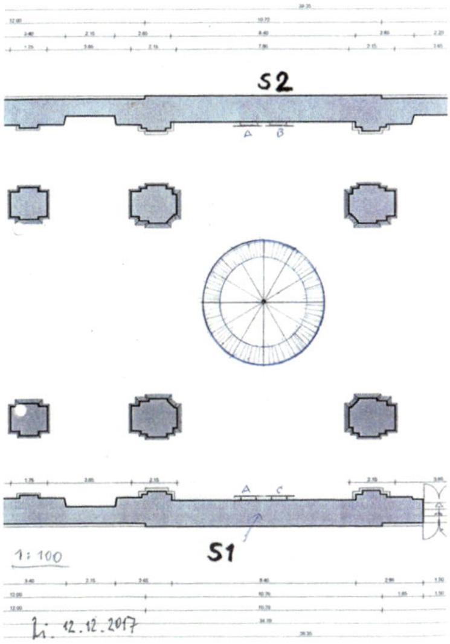

FIG. 29

Drawing of the internal divisions of the plane of oscillation, December 2017

FIG. 30

Drawing showing the positions of the double mirrors and the plane of oscillation, 12 December 2017

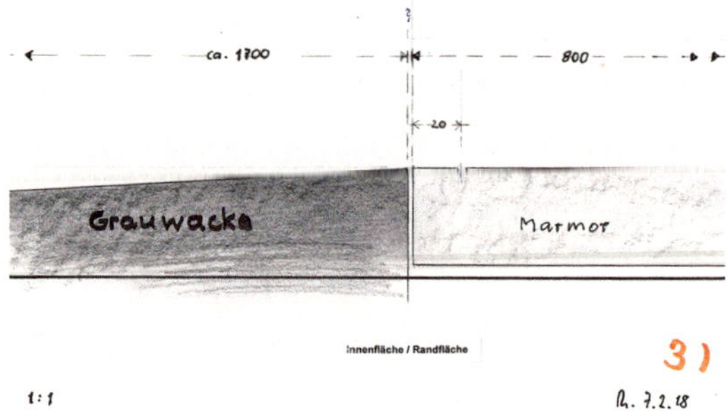

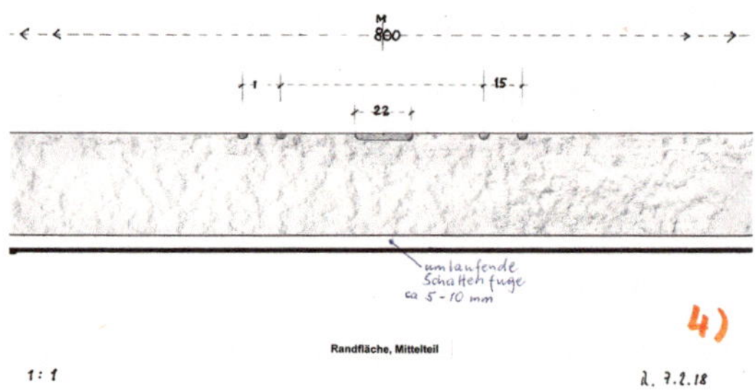

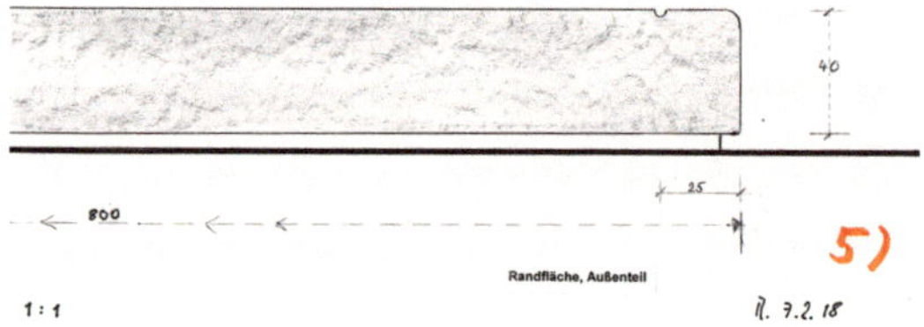

FIGS. 31–33

Drawing showing the materials and the structure of the plane of oscillation, 7 February 2018

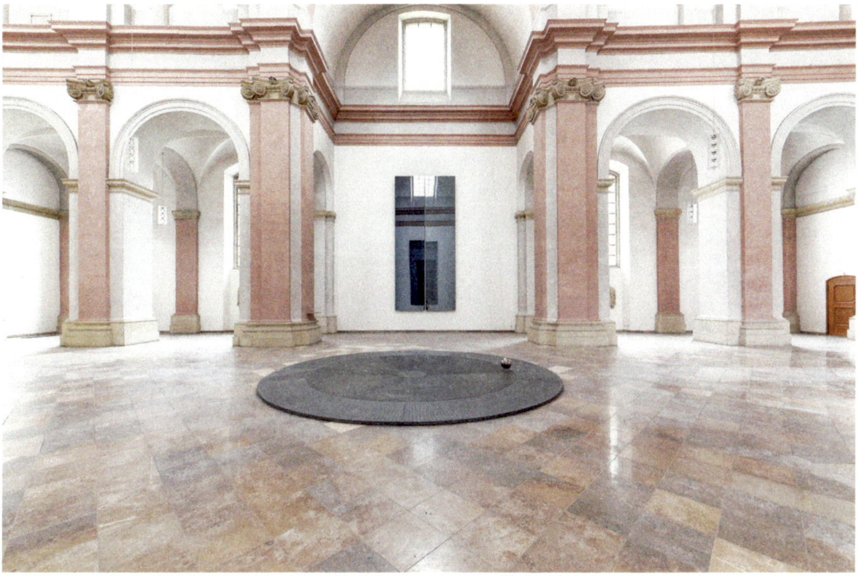

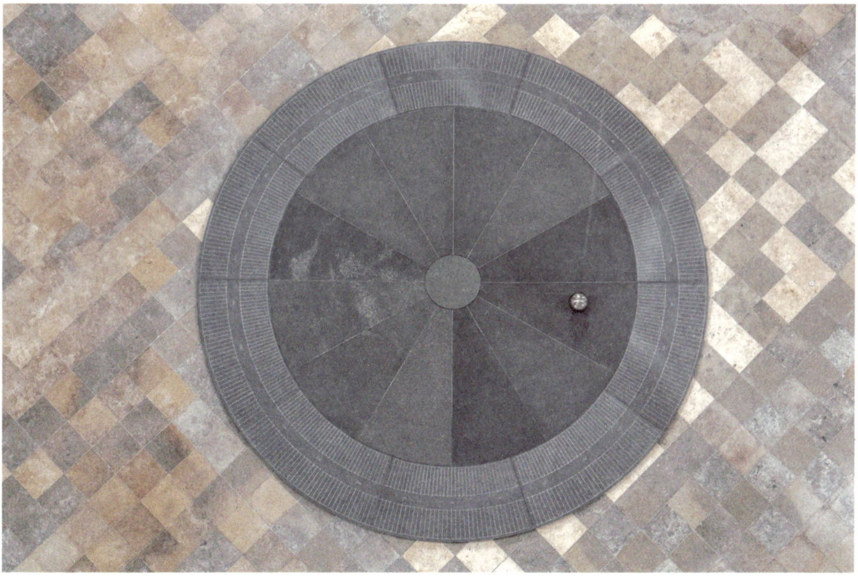

FIGS. 34 and 35

The pendulum and the plane of oscillation in the Dominikanerkirche, 2018

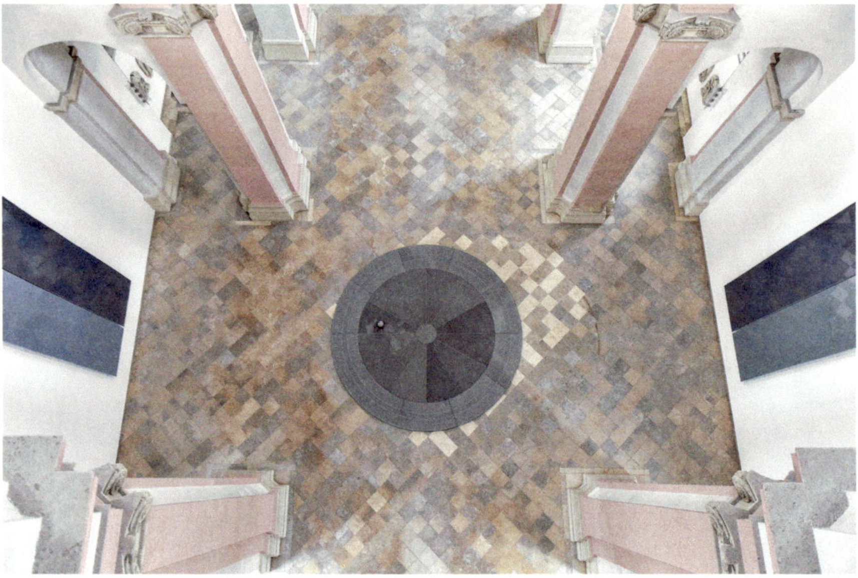

FIG. 36

View from above of the pendulum and the plane of oscillation in the Dominikanerkirche, 2018

The Work and the Facts

As the title of the work indicates, the pendulum takes centre stage with the double mirrors in supporting roles. Thus there is an encounter between two elements that make no attempt to conceal their different characters – Foucault's pendulum borrowed from the history of science and the mirror objects created by the artist. Richter places these elements in separate locations, giving each its own status. He neither melds them into a single entity that wholly subsumes them nor does he make anything of the provocative confrontation of the realms of science and art within which the elements function and are perceived. While the pendulum quantifies the vertical dimension of the space, the mirrors operate in a horizontal dimension, reflecting what happens between them. Since the viewer's perceptions of the mirrors follow a familiar aesthetic trajectory, the main question arising from the work concerns the presence of a scientific instrument within a work of art.

Much earlier in his career Richter had already – rather ambivalently – made a note concerning factual reality as it is portrayed by science. Science's efforts to explain things instilled in him a sense of the truly overwhelming nature of that which has not yet been explained and prompted him to intentionally ignore the latter: "The sciences certainly have influenced the arts. To an Aztec, the sunset was an inexplicable event, which he could not cope with or even survive without the imagined aid of his gods. Obvious phenomena of this sort have since been explained. But the sheer unimagined vastness of the explicable has now made the inexplicable into such a monstrous thing that our heads spin, and the old images burst like bubbles. The thought of the totally inexplicable (as when we look at the starry sky), and the impossibility of reading any sense into this monstrous vastness, so affect us that we need ignorance to survive."[16]

A note from a good twenty years later reflects Richter's unremitting interest in science as a critical discipline that takes on reality and never shrouds it in ideological assertions: "My profound distaste for all claims to possess the truth, and for all ideologies . . . now receives confirmation from such people as the physicist Dürr, the evolutionary scientist Riedland, and Konrad Lorenz, who say that our sole hope of survival lies in the 'gropings of human self-doubt': in our awareness of our own limitations. And so I hope that my 'incapacity' – the scepticism that stands in for capacity – may after all turn out to be an important 'modern' strategy for humankind. Even more than before, therefore, I can assume (and, where possible, proclaim)

16 "Notes, 1962", in Gerhard Richter, *Text 1961–2007: Writings, Interviews and Letters,* ed. Dietmar Elger and Hans Ulrich Obrist (London: Thames & Hudson, 2009), p. 15 (hereafter abbreviated as *Text*).

that the absurdity (and inhumanity) of all ideology is a given fact."[17]

Richter does not regard the sciences as the antithesis to agnostic doubt in the feasibility of knowledge creation; in his view they make the link between a capacity to research and comprehensive doubt and self-criticism. This is not some blanket faith in science; Richter is also no fan of the scientization of art or of using art to illustrate science, as practiced by Gruppe Zero or as seen in the art and technology programme of the Los Angeles County Museum of Art and in recent spectacular museum events. For Richter science is not just a point of reference that the artist can look to, he also sees it as analogous to art, insofar as science is driven by the desire to define a reality of its own that is unmuddied by ideological claims. In response to a question from Irmeline Lebeer in an interview in 1973, when she asked if he regarded painting as "an expression of self", Richter refuted the idea and instead described painting "as an autonomous reality, with no relation to any given reality except itself."[18] On that basis painting should generate a structure whose internal laws and harmonies are sufficient unto themselves. Since making that statement Richter has returned to the same idea from time to time, on one occasion in connection with painting as an analogy to music by Johann Sebastian Bach: "I'm thinking here of Bach's *Well-Tempered Clavier* and a comment on it

---

17 "Notes, 1988", in *Text*, p. 200.

18 "Interview with Irmeline Lebeer" [1973], in *Text*, p. 79.

that this is such perfect music that it doesn't need us any more."[19]

However, self-sufficient perfection can find itself in danger of tipping into mechanical sequences. In Richter's *Atlas*, a collection of photographs, drawings, sketches, and other documents that has evolved with his work, there is a set of sketches arising from numerical sequences.[20] Evidently Richter was attracted by the idea of basing linear and planar compositions on law-abiding numerical sequences. However, he stopped short of creating any paintings based on these sketches since he soon realized that a process of that kind could descend into trivia. On the basis that a numerical sequence is a factual component – as opposed to subjective compositional invention – it is clear that Richter considered very carefully which or what kind of facts could be of use to him. A painting does not come about of its own accord and its success is entirely dependent on the decisions the artist makes.

Ever since the mid-twentieth century any object that is sourced in the real world and incorporated into a work

---

19 Gerhard Richter, in Gerhard Richter and Dieter Schwarz, *Ein Gespräch / An Interview*. Dresden: Staatliche Kunstsammlungen (Dresden and Cologne: Verlag der Buchhandlung Walther König, 2019) (= Schriften des Gerhard Richter Archiv Dresden, 17), p. 30.

20 Gerhard Richter, *Atlas* (Munich: Städtische Galerie im Lenbachhaus and Cologne: Verlag der Buchhandlung Walther König, 2015), pp. 268–71 (hereafter abbreviated as *Atlas*).

of art is immediately labelled a "readymade". But is it right to categorize the pendulum as a readymade – when Marcel Duchamp coined that term for a very particular practice? As Duchamp used the term, a readymade is any object whatsoever that is selected – regardless of its aesthetics – and designated a "work of art". As Duchamp himself said: "The choice was based on a reaction of *visual* indifference with at the same time a total absence of good or bad taste … in fact a complete anaesthesia."[21] Having been extracted from ordinary life and declared a work of art, the object in question now functioned in an aesthetic context; it derived its meaning from the claim made by the artist – not from any of its existing qualities, either visible or innate. For the viewer the visual shock was compounded by the semantic shock, all the more so since Duchamp's gesture not only

---

21 "Ce choix était fondé sur une réaction d'indifference *visuelle*, assortie au même moment à une absence totale de bon ou mauvais goût… en fait une anesthésie complete." Marcel Duchamp, "A propos des Ready-mades" [1961], in Marcel Duchamp, *Duchamp du signe: Écrits*. Réunis et présentés par Michel Sanouillet. Nouvelle édition revue et augmentée avec la collaboration de Elmer Peterson. Paris: Flammarion, 1975, p. 191. English in The Art of Assemblage: A Symposium, The Museum of Modern Art, New York, October 19, 1961. Marcel Duchamp, "Apropos of 'Readymades,'" talk delivered by Duchamp as a panel member of the "Art of Assemblage" symposium at the Museum of Modern Art, New York, 19 October 1961. Published in *Art and Artists*, (July 1966), 47, and reprinted in *Salt Seller. The Writings of Marcel Duchamp (Marchand du Sel)*, ed. Michel Sanouillet and Elmer Peterson (New York: Oxford University Press, 1973).

rebuffed any kind of formal, historical, or iconographic interpretation, it by definition negated the latter.

None of that applies to Richter's work. While the pendulum is not in itself primarily remarkable for its visual properties, it gains an aesthetic presence by virtue of the choices Richter made for this work and for its presentation. What matters here above all is the facticity of the pendulum, which – regardless of any kinds of considerations or contemporary opinions – steadily adheres to a path solely determined by physical forces. The pendulum that Richter has introduced into this work of art is an immutable fact; it serves as a *tertium comparationis*, an independent point of reference. There are echoes here of a goal Richter already set for himself as a young man: "Sacrifice oneself to objectivity." And he continued, rather polemically: "I have always loathed subjectivity. Even failure, poor quality, opportunism and lack of character are a small price to pay in order to produce something objective, definitive, universal, right."[22] When he made those comments he may already have been anticipating his Grey Paintings, which we will return to in due course here.

There is one work by Duchamp that specifically refers to science and can illuminate Richter's different relationship to science. Duchamp's *Trois stoppages-étalon (Three Standard Stoppages)* (1913–14) is the outcome of an experiment he devised – "Un mètre de fil droit, horizontal, tombé d'un mètre de haut" ("A straight horizontal thread one metre in length dropped from a height of one metre") –

[22] "Notes, 1973", in Gerhard Richter, *Text*, p. 70.

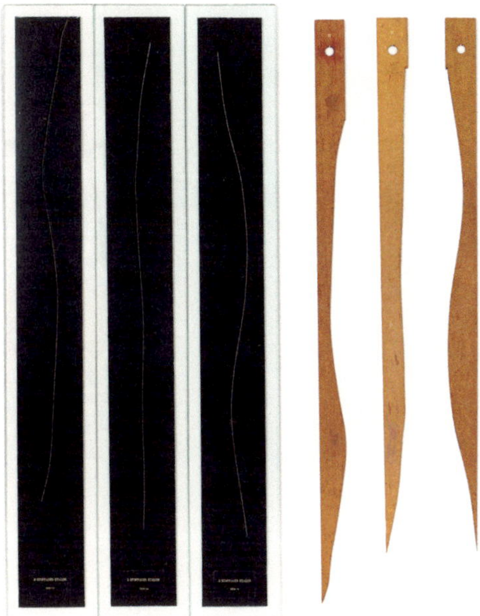

Marcel Duchamp, *Trois Stoppages-étalon* (*Three Standard Stoppages*), 1913–1914. The Museum of Modern Art, New York, Katherine S. Dreier Bequest

and executed by allowing each of the three threads to fall onto a strip of canvas in exactly that manner. He recorded the results of the experiment – the three shapes made by the threads – and had three "measuring sticks" made with one side of each replicating the curved line of the thread. Now the random shapes could be reproduced at will. It is not by chance that these three lengths of wood are reminiscent of the standard metre that is preserved in Paris as a universal reference. At the same time, the accidental

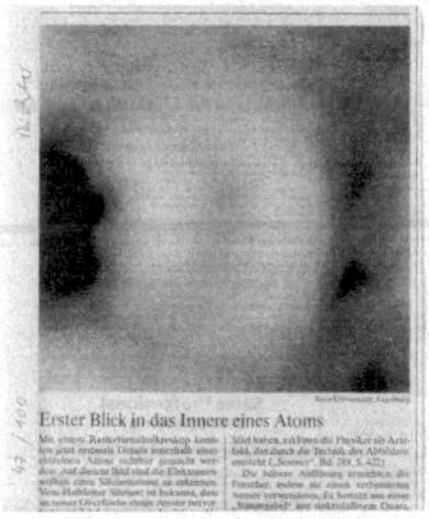

Gerhard Richter, *Erster Blick*, 2000
Offset print on paper, mounted on card, 18.2 × 15.1 cm

nature of their origin makes it impossible to credit them with any particular validity beyond that of their individual existences. Duchamp's *Trois stoppages-étalon* represent the rejection of any kind of transferable knowledge, they are a manifesto for an art that does away with both formal and discursive conventions; moreover, as pseudo-instruments they are distinct from contemporary pictorial or plastic works of art, such as sculptures. They enter the world – specifically the art world – as unique, non-negotiable, inapplicable facts.

By contrast Richter availed himself of an established experiment that no-one can cast doubt on and utilized the pendulum as the main component in a multipart work, without alienating it from its original function. His use of a pendulum is entirely free of the polemical overtones that Duchamp intended in his work; unlike Duchamp, Richter is not seeking to take a stand against modernist or post-modernist sculpture. And this introduction of a pendulum into a work of art is not the first time that Richter has incorporated a factual component into a piece or has even directly declared that component to be the work. A few instances of this may serve to illustrate this aspect of his work. The main focus in all of these is not on science but on facticity, on something with its own existence that might be detached from the factual "crowd" in the way that Richter has variously used private or found photographs as the basis for oil paintings.

In 2000 Richter made a print replicating a photograph of the electron cloud around a silicon atom taken with an atomic force microscope and published in the *Frankfurter Allgemeine Zeitung*. The newspaper cutting was reproduced unchanged in the offset print and the title, *Erster Druck* (*First View*) was taken from the headline above the article telling readers that this was the "first view of the interior of an atom."[23] A continuation of this idea is seen in the group of Silicate paintings done in 2003 and in the subsequent paintings based on enlargements of molecular

[23] *Gerhard Richter: Editionen 1965–2013*, ed. Hubertus Butin, Stefan Gronert, and Thomas Olbricht (Ostfildern: Hatje Cantz Verlag, 2014), no. 112 (hereafter abbreviated as Butin + number).

structures. Richter later recalled how he had chanced upon a nano-technological illustration one day when he was reading the *Frankfurter Allgemeine Zeitung*: "And when I found that image in a newspaper, it was like a gift. That is how the four large paintings came about. I called them *Structures*, *Structures 1–4*, because I didn't understand anything at all of what they depicted, that's to say, I knew next to nothing about silicates. But by now I'm so much more familiar with them that I have used the title *Silicate*. Later on I came across another, very attractive structure – the structure of strontium."[24] The sheet of structures in Richter's *Atlas*[25] conveys a sense of the way (reminiscent of the numerical sequences mentioned earlier here) that Richter, responding to the ambivalence of the structures in these images, decided to work with just one of them. However, he did not use a photo-mechanical technique to reproduce these structures – as he had done for the offset print – but instead painted them in an even greater magnification in his *Silicate* paintings.[26] These large, wall-sized

24 "Interview mit Benjamin H. D. Buchloh" [2004], in Gerhard Richter, *Text 1961 bis 2007: Schriften, Interviews, Briefe*, ed. Dietmar Elger and Hans Ulrich Obrist (Cologne: Verlag der Buchhandlung Walther König, 2008, p. 495 [trans. for this essay].

25 *Atlas*, p. 743.

26 Dietmar Elger, *Gerhard Richter: Catalogue raisonné*, ed. Staatliche Kunstsammlungen Dresden, Gerhard Richter Archiv. vols. 1–5 (Ostfildern: Hatje Cantz Verlag, 2011–20), nos. 885/1–4 (hereafter abbreviated as Elger + number).

formats depict four different electron-microscope images that arose from the three-dimensional molecular structure being shifted and turned around. Each painting comprises a detail of a potentially infinite structure; at the end of the painting process a soft brush was used to gently blur the image, so that – for all the accuracy of the drawing – the surface lost its graphic look and took on a more solidly grey appearance. Next came *Strontium*, a monumental composition put together from 130 photographs and measuring over nine by nine metres, which was installed in the new entrance hall of the De Young Museum in San Francisco.[27] Variants on this image in *Atlas* show how Richter removed the opposition of figure and ground by adjusting the focus of the image, ultimately creating an even spread of image noise where no single element stands out too much.[28]

Unlike the paintings done after photographs of figures, objects, or landscapes, the contents of these images are both abstract and concrete, that is to say, a molecule that is omnipresent in our world yet impossible to see with the naked eye. Selecting and illustrating this fact neither enlightens the viewer nor does it create new meaning – it is simply a fact of life, it is not making a statement. Basically it is tautologous: the fact confirms its own existence but does not comment on it. This fact is a piece of unalterable reality, something real, and – for whatever reason, be it

27 Elger 888.

28 *Atlas*, pp. 745–48.

confidence or despair – we, artists and viewers alike, try to turn it into a picture.

There is something in the selection of a fact of this kind that allows it to be seen as a metaphor. This sets it apart from the readymade, which – leaving aside its capacity to provoke – lacks the required pictoriality, or rather, the readymade has deliberately been stripped of its pictoriality. By dint of their monotony – their endless repetition of identical shapes – the structures Richter saw and selected negate any promise inherent in nature: they loom into view as images of nothingness. When Benjamin Buchloh suggested to Richter that there was scepticism, even hopelessness in his *Structures*, Richter agreed: "I have also thought, at times, that perhaps this really is quite a terrifying thematic, like getting closer to the end, in the direction of death and dissolution, down to the very elements, where all that is left are these dread atomic structures."[29] However, Richter made nothing of the fact that these compositions are about molecular structures; instead he compared them with some of his early paintings with repetitive motifs – his paintings of tubes, corrugated iron, doors, windows, curtains, beams.[30] Like the molecular structures these motifs have a tendency towards the ornamental, but they also still retain an element of illusion, that leap from illusion to disillusion, when the implied

---

29 "Interview with Benjamin H. D. Buchloh" [2004], in *Text*, p. 486.

30 Elger 158, 159, 161, 162, 163-1, 163-2, 204, 205, 207, 208-1, 208-2, 209-8.

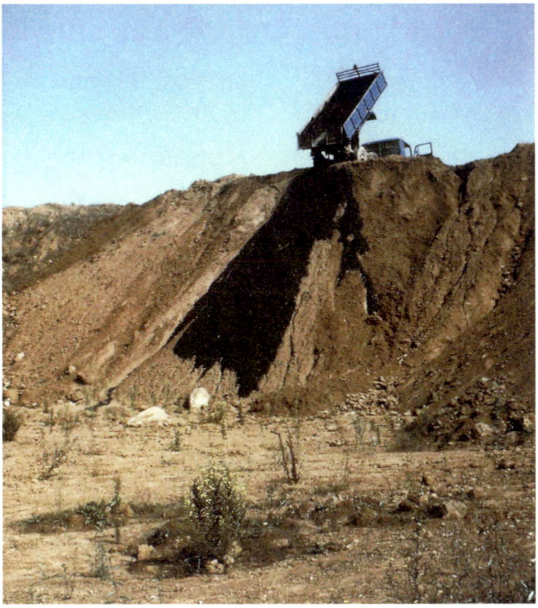

Robert Smithson, *Asphalt Rundown*, Rome, October 1969

sight of something behind the motif is rebuffed by an opaque surface.

Like the *Structures*, the pendulum is strictly regular in its movements and in its repetition which leads nowhere other than back to itself. Although the pendulum, as an object, is perfectly visible, its relationship to the rotation of the Earth is not directly perceptible – it can only ever be established in retrospect because the rotation proceeds too slowly for the eye to take in. Unlike the rotating Earth and the ever-changing phenomena reflected in the mirrors, the pendulum – regardless of its physical definition – represents reliable constancy.

There is an interesting comparison to be made here between Richter's just letting things happen and the factuality that informed so much American art in the 1960s. Still in the realm of familiar scientific facts, the work of Robert Smithson suffices as an example given that he made direct reference to physical laws, which he regarded and presented as analogous to artistic deliberations. In some works Smithson set processes in motion, which – given that particular situation – then develop of their own accord and in their own way demonstrate a recurrent theme in Smithson's work, namely the transition from order to a less ordered state. This is seen for instance in his *Asphalt Rundown* (1969), which resulted from asphalt being poured down an earthy slope; it is also seen in similar processes involving liquid concrete and glue (*Concrete Pour*, *Glue Pour*), and ultimately in the construction of *Spiral Jetty*. The predictable destruction of this work by natural forces stands as a symbol of the unstoppable reduction of every kind of order to entropy.[31] The processes in Smithson's works always have a defined goal; they lead from one state to another and, in so doing, create a model of an onward flow that both embraces the history of the Earth and points to the future. There is no such teleology in Richter's work. On the contrary, he presents us with facts – without comment – that, unaffected by change (of whatever kind) stand solely on their own account.

---

31 Robert Hobbs, *Robert Smithson: Sculpture*, with contributions by Lawrence Alloway, John Coplans, Lucy R. Lippard (Ithaca, NY, and London: Cornell University Press, 1981), nos. 52, 54, 56 and 61.

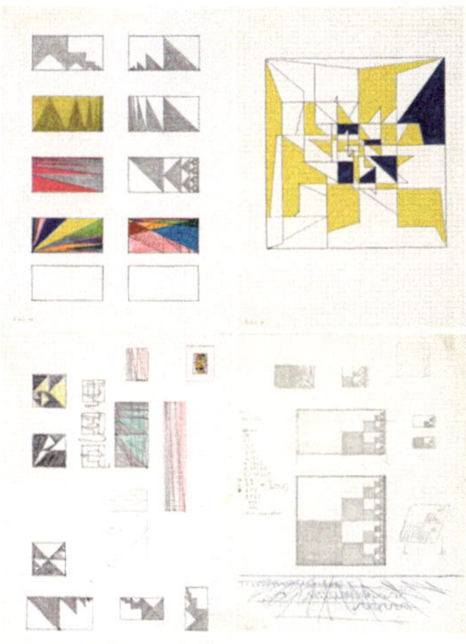

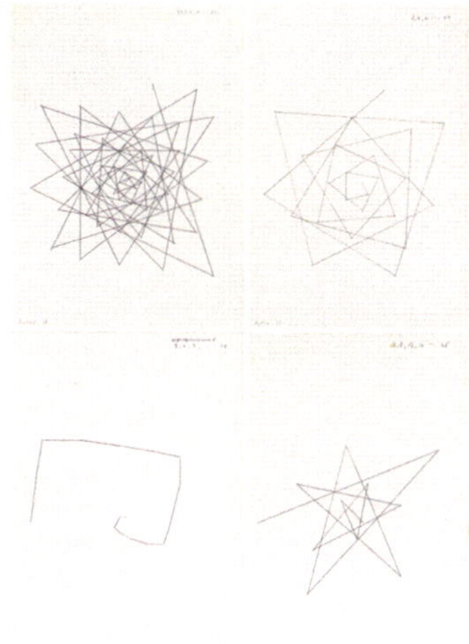

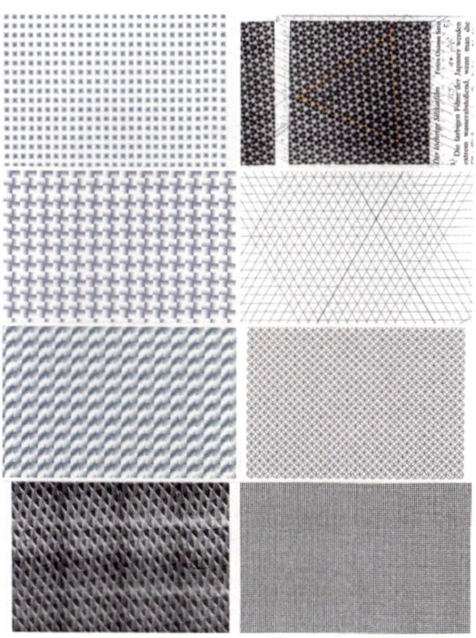

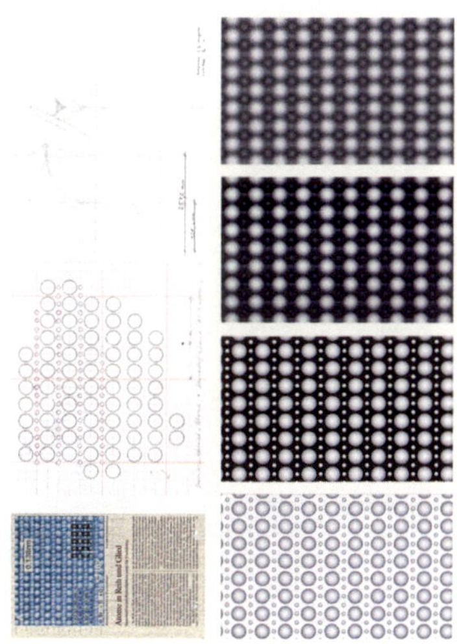

FIGS. 37 and 38

Sketches (Numbers), *Atlas,* sheets 268 and 269, ca. 1978

FIGS. 39 and 40

Various Structures and Silicate, *Atlas,* sheet 743;
Strontium, *Atlas,* sheet 745, 2006

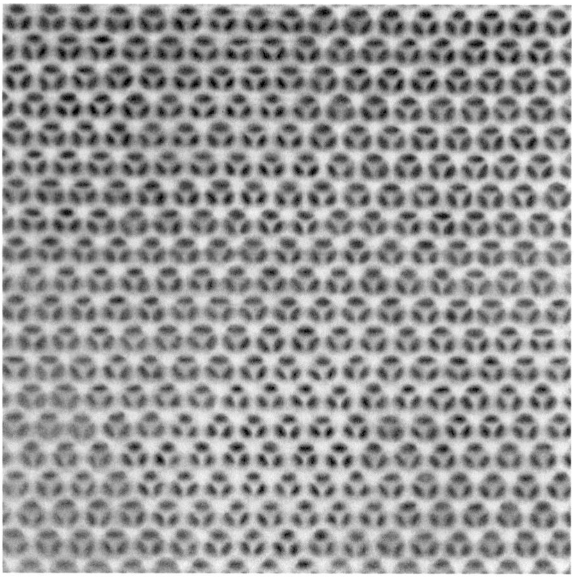

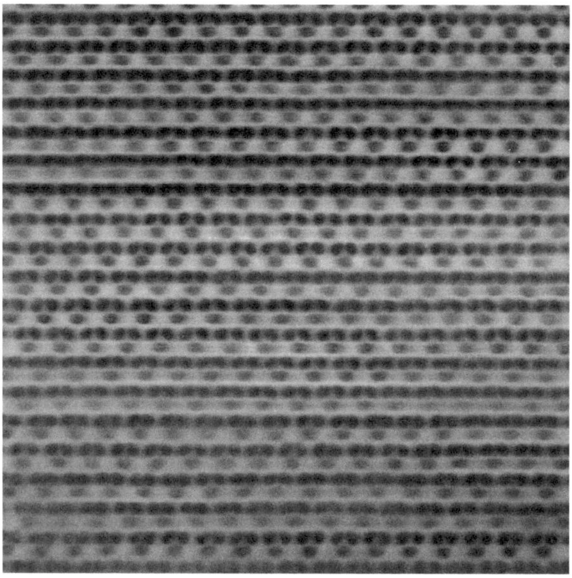

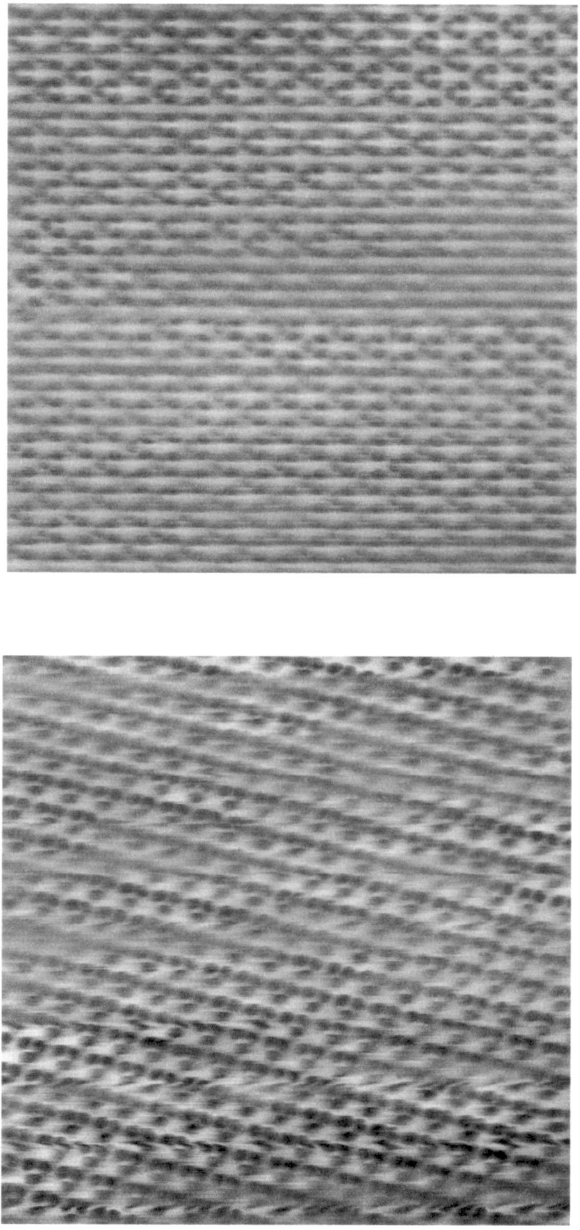

FIG. 41

Silicate 1–4 (885/1–4), 2003

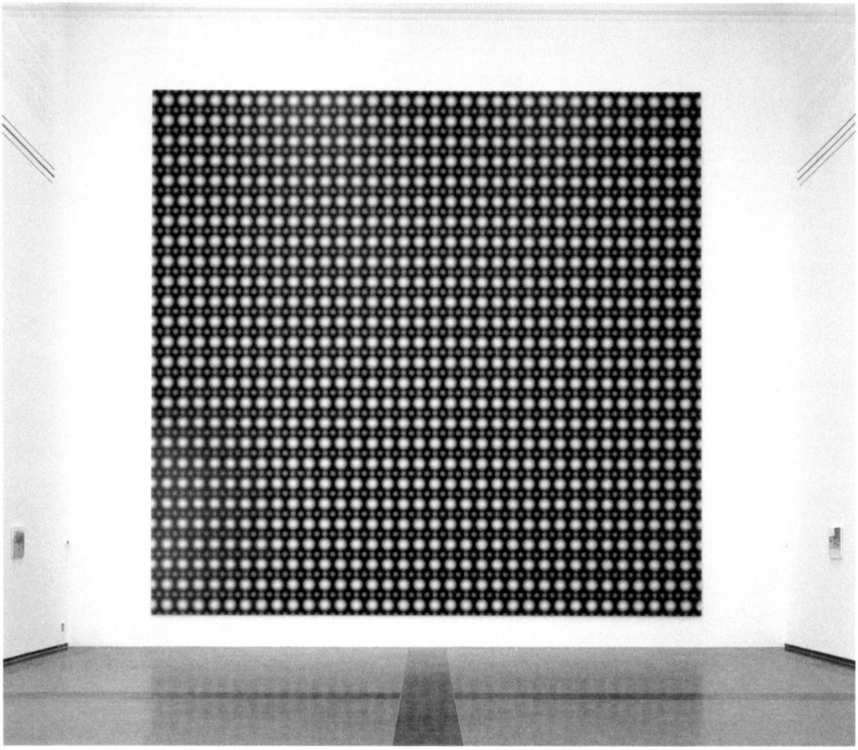

FIG. 42

Strontium (888), 2004,
in K20, Kunstsammlung Nordrhein-Westfalen,
Düsseldorf, 2005

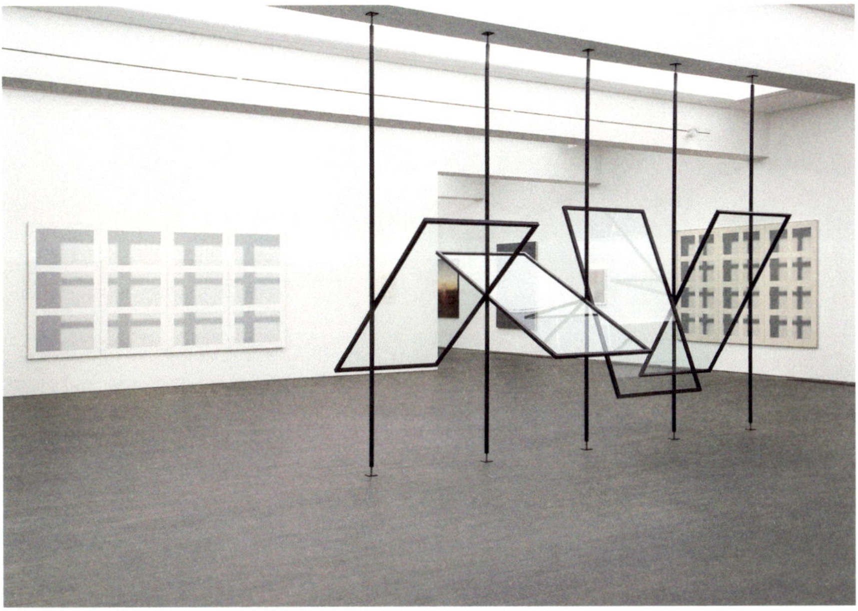

FIG. 43

Window (205), 1968, and *Window Grid* (207), 1968,
with *4 Panes of Glass* (160), 1967, in S.M.A.K., Ghent, 2017

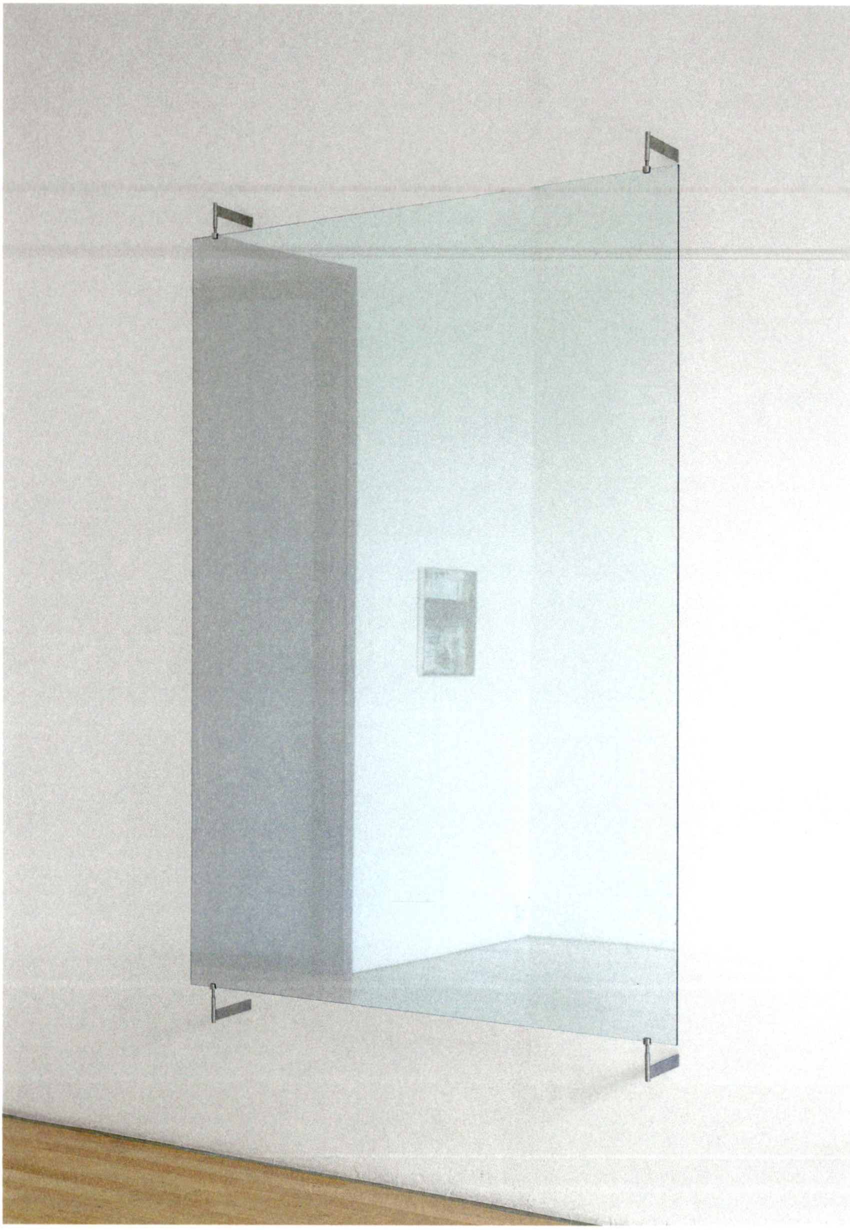

FIG. 44

Pane of Glass (876/1), 2002

Glass

Around the time that Richter painted his *Structures*, he also made two versions of a prism, which came out as a multiple in 2002.[32] As so often in his long career, Richter chose to make a fundamental statement via a multiple, purportedly produced as an occasional edition. The two prisms are solid glass bodies in the form of an elongated equilateral triangle, with no hint of any intervention or addition by the artist. The only decisions made by Richter were the dimensions of the prisms and their protection in presentation cases. A prism refracts any beam of light entering and exiting it, and if that beam falls on a neutral surface, its colour spectrum fans out into its rainbow hues.

Richter's choice of a geometric body reminds the viewer of that effect, but he does not use it to create a spectacular effect or as a didactic scientific exercise. Richter merely points to the refraction of light as the physical basis of our perception of colours. By merely pointing to something he respects the presence and immutability of the factual order that we participate in and that we depend on in our daily lives without necessarily either knowing or understanding how it works. In that sense the choice of a

[32] Butin 120 and 121.

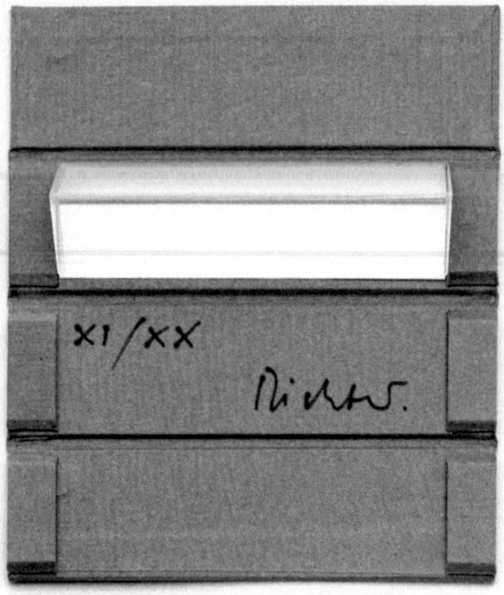

Gerhard Richter, *Prism I,* 2002,
prism of colourless heavy flint glass
in folding case, 16 × 4.7 × 4.1 cm (prism)

prism was not entirely innocuous, because colour perception is fundamental to painting. In the same way that the world is largely based on silicates, the production and appreciation of paintings relies on the refraction of light into colours – were it not for that it would be impossible to differentiate what we see in the visible world.

This little work is related to the works using clear panes of glass that Richter started to develop in 2002. Fascinated by the properties of glass, which is transparent yet also has the capacity to produce stronger or weaker reflections, Richter now started to present panes of glass, singly or in groups, without subjecting them to any artistic treatment. On the contrary glass, as opposed to canvas, wood, and paper, is not the obvious choice as a picture carrier because its solid, hard surface cannot easily be used for pictorial representation. At that time Richter had not yet started to work with coloured glass as an artistic material as he would do some years later when he created a stained-glass window for Cologne Cathedral. The only intervention he did make was to have some of the panes of glass professionally treated with a fine coating that slightly enhanced their reflectivity.

An early group of twelve single panes of glass in a variety of formats allowed Richter to explore differences in the look of the transparent surfaces depending on how they were mounted on the wall.[33] These were followed by panes of glass standing upright (in a support) in the space – four at first, then five, seven, and even nine, with the result that the level of transparency was progressively reduced and viewers saw multiple reflections of themselves.[34] In 2003 Richter created a number of glass compositions consisting of different-sized sets of eleven tightly packed, vertical-format panes of glass propped up against a wall.[35] The slight angle and the layering of the panes of glass meant that viewers saw multiply refracted versions of their own images and of the surroundings – with blurred outlines and rather grey, like reminders of Richter's blurred paint

33 Elger 876/1–12.

34 Elger 877/1–2, 879/1–4.

35 Elger 886/1–5.

finishes. These two presentation modes then came together in 2012 in Richter's *8 Panes*, with each of the upstanding eight panes – one behind the other – tilting slightly backwards or forwards.[36] The final statement in this group came in the sequence of panes that Richter created in 2015 – *14 Panes of Glass for Toyoshima, Dedicated to Futility* – for the island pavilion on Toyoshima (mentioned earlier here) with its open views out to sea. Here the viewer's gaze does not travel through mildly reflective panes of glass to the evenly lit walls of an exhibition space, but rather out to the landscape, to bamboo groves and water in the changing light of the seasons and of the times of day. The spatial situation, the work, and the surroundings become a single, harmonious entity.[37]

Richter's interest in the properties of clear panes of glass goes all the way back to his *4 Panes* (1967).[38] These four panes in metal frames are arranged side-by-side, fixed between floor-to-ceiling metal uprights but able to rotate on their fixings. Whatever position they are given, they basically only ever show what is behind them. Evidently the symbolic power of this work had played a part in Richter calculations from the outset, given that he described the complete transparency suggested by this work as both

---

36 Elger 928.

37 Elger 942. On this, see *Gerhard Richter: 14 Panes of Glass for Toyoshima, Dedicated to Futility* (Tokyo: Wako Works of Art, 2016).

38 Elger 160.

illuminating and devastating – that which is perceived through the glass sinks into indifference. He made a telling note on a drawing of this glass wall: "Glass symbol (see everything understand nothing)".[39]

The demise of understanding marks an extreme in Richter's confrontation with the fact of glass. However, in recent years (as we have seen) Richter has shifted the focus from the blunt unambiguity of transparent glass to the ambivalence of reflective glass. This also means that the concentration on the supposedly immediately apparent reality behind the glass shifted into a form of contemplation that takes in several layers, that is to say, the image behind the glass plus the medium of glass as such plus the reflection of what is happening in front of the glass. And that brings us back to the situation in Münster and raises the question as to the potentially metaphorical nature of that work.

---

39 "Glas Symbol (alles sehen nichts begreifen)": Dieter Schwarz, *Gerhard Richter: Zeichnungen 1964–1999. Werkverzeichnis*, with an essay by Birgit Pelzer (Winterthur: Kunstmuseum Winterthur and Düsseldorf: Richter Verlag, 1999), no. 66/8.

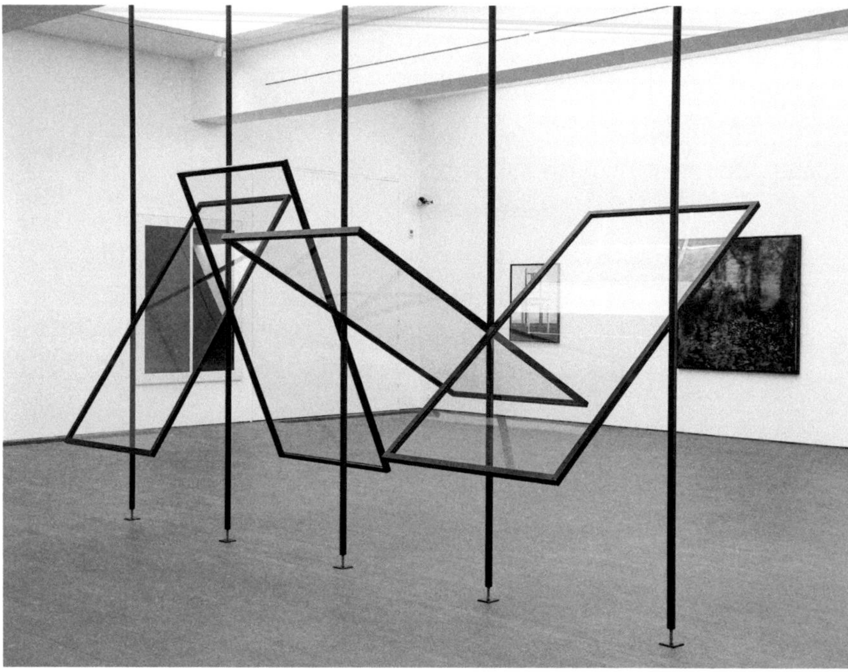

FIG. 45
4 Panes of Glass (160), 1967, in S.M.A.K., Ghent, 2017

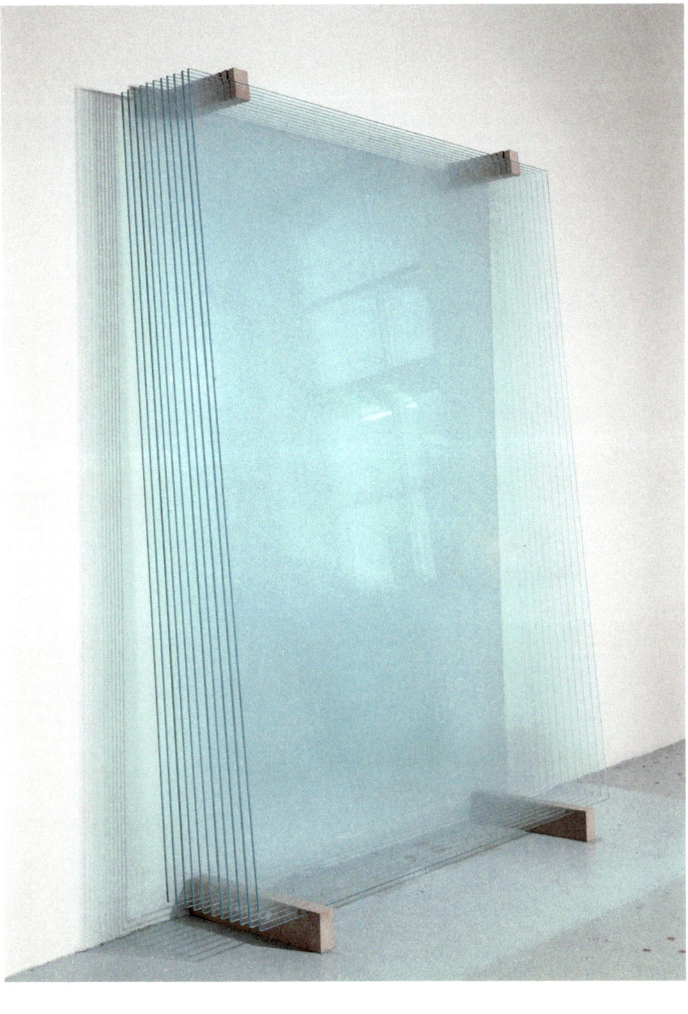

FIG. 46

11 Panes (886/1), 2003

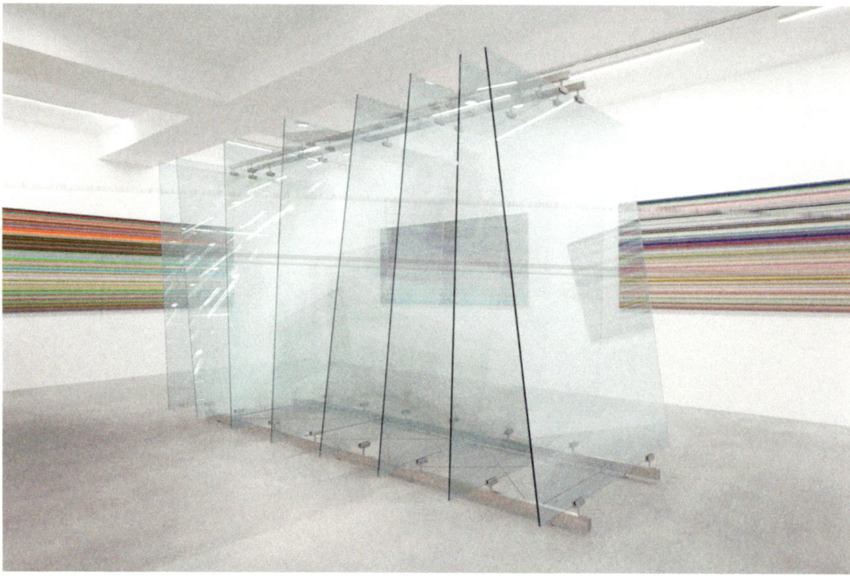

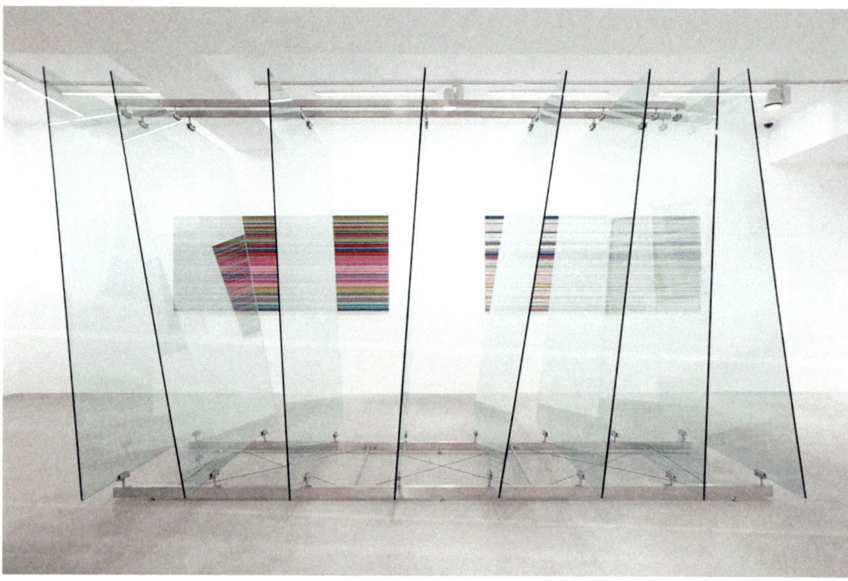

FIGS. 47 a and b
8 Panes (928), 2012

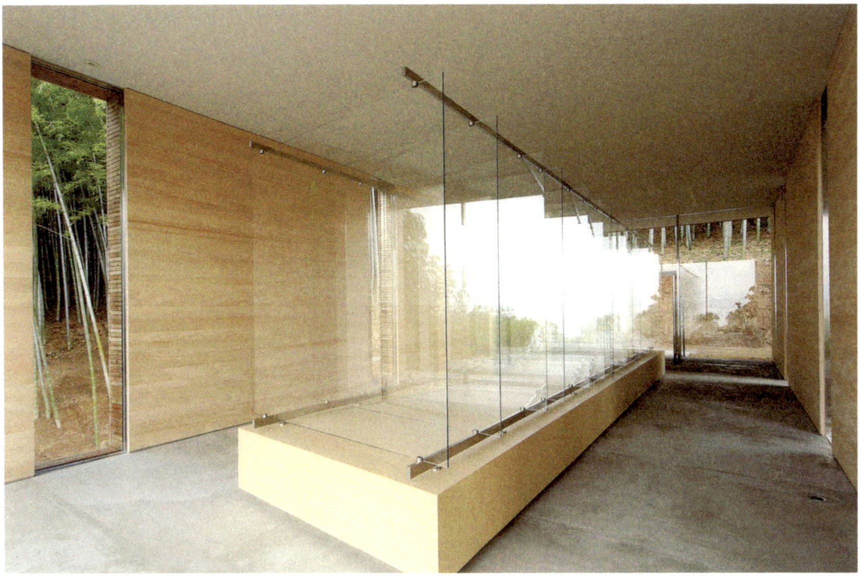

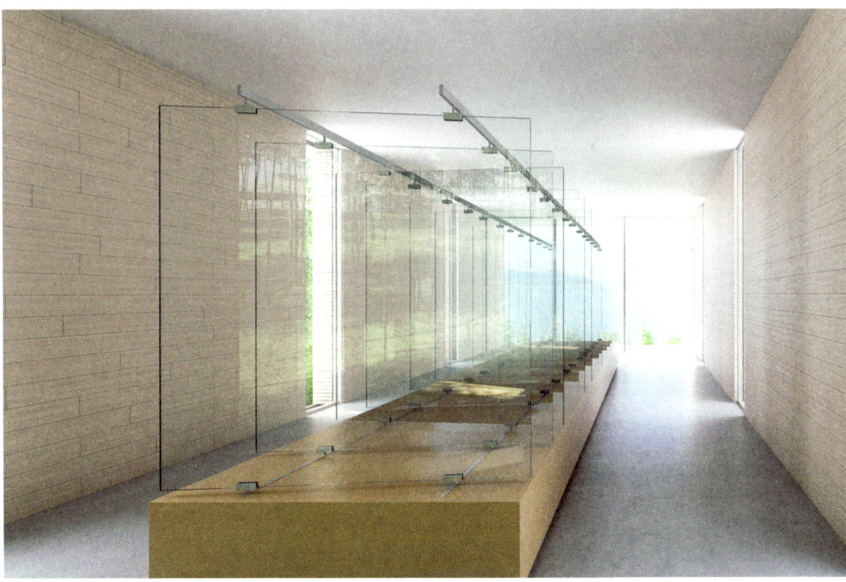

FIGS. 48 a and b

14 Panes of Glass for Toyoshima, (dedicated to futility) (942), 2015

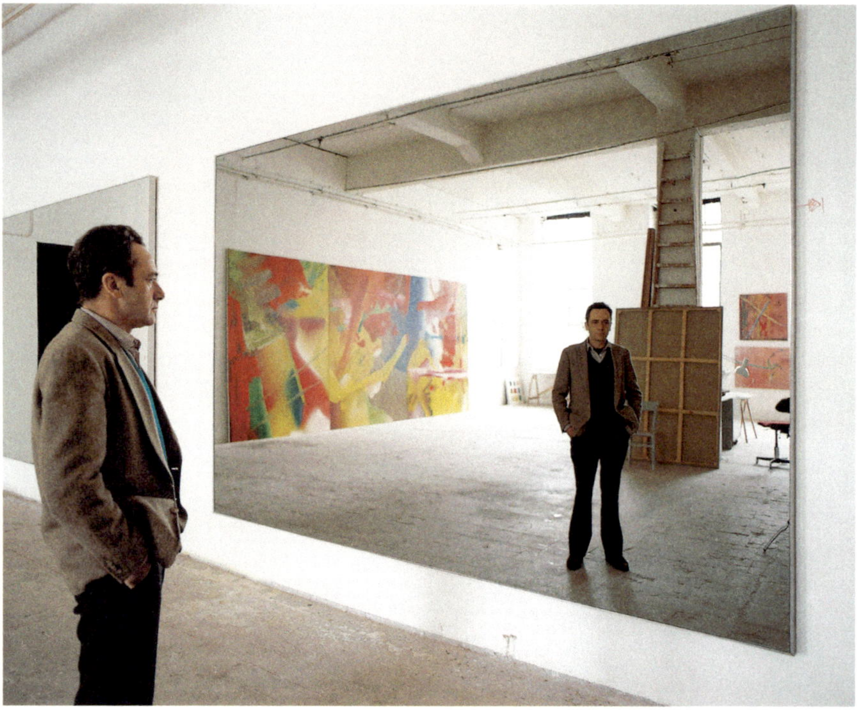

FIG. 49
Mirrors (470/1 and 2), 1981

Mirrors

The counterpart to the panes of glass is the reflective metal sphere. "We would all come to an agreement, once and for all, on the sphere. At home, I have these particularly beautiful steel balls. It's impossible to get any closer to perfection. But if we start down that path, it's all over."[40] That was Richter's response to Irmeline Lebeer in the interview (mentioned earlier here) she conducted with him in 1973, when she asked if he were striving for perfection or for dynamics and tension. That was not just the end of that topic, the interview also came to an end – there was nowhere to go after the perfect sphere.

In Richter's *Atlas* there is a group of photographs taken in 1968 when he was experimenting with metal spheres and utilizing their comprehensively reflective, unlimited surfaces.[41] Two decades later the sphere appeared in his work as a real object when the Anthony d'Offay Gallery in London released an edition of 25 solid, stainless steel spheres measuring 8 cm in diameter. These were polished steel spheres made for industrial use by the

---

40 "Interview with Irmeline Lebeer" [1973], in *Text*, p. 83.

41 *Atlas*, p. 81.

specialist ball-bearing manufacturers Kugelfischer in Germany. In 1992 the same gallery released an edition of a steel sphere with a diameter of 16 centimetres.[42] Richter likes placing a sphere on the studio floor, in front of paintings; as it rolls around it creates ever-new reflections of its surroundings. Unlike the first set of untitled spheres, each of the eleven exemplars of the later edition are engraved with the name of a Swiss mountain in the Upper Engadine. The decision to do that was inspired by holidays Richter had spent there in the village of Sils-Maria. In the case of the sphere engraved with that name, the reference to nature and the mirror motif meet. The sphere is the epitome of a mirror, with its hard, gleaming surface reflecting everything that happens around it; there is no point in the surroundings that is not reflected in its surface. It has no fixed position, no place, no above and no below. Its interior is inaccessible, its reflective exterior is pure illusion. Meanwhile the mountains that give the spheres their names are just as inaccessible, only in a different way, that is to say, as representatives of a natural world that is as sublime as it is hostile, because they embody not an illusion but a reality that overpowers the individual. Both the reflective sphere and the mountains have that inescapable, factual quality that has already been mentioned here, and in that sense they paved the way for Richter's use of a pendulum.

---

42 Butin 76 and 77.

Clearly Richter recognized the pictorial potential of the self-generating reflections on the movable panes of glass and later returned to that phenomenon. In 1981, for instance, he identified a simple crystal mirror with a plain wooden frame as a picture and hung it in an exhibition at Kunsthalle Düsseldorf; a few years later he used it as a cover picture for a monograph on his work.[43] The cover shows Richter standing in front of two extremely large mirrors in the same formats, which reflect the interior of the studio and open up a strangely flat picture plane bereft of perspective. As it were standing in for the viewer, Richter demonstrates the intimate relationship between the viewer and the picture plane that immediately occurs when someone looks into a mirror and which ends again as soon as the viewer departs. In the reflection the person gazing into the mirror becomes an object that is the same distance away from the viewer as the reflected paintings and objects. This is merely an indication of "the fact that every picture is a mirror" and that every picture is thus "an appearance and an illusion, however radical it may be".[44]

Like the transparent glass panes from 1967 the crystal mirrors are aggressively hard. Nothing about them lessens

---

43 Elger 470-1. The monograph in question is Ulrich Loock and Denys Zacharopoulos, *Gerhard Richter* (Munich: Verlag Silke Schreiber, 1985).

44 "Interview with Hans-Ulrich Obrist" [1993], in *Text*, p. 305.

the harshness of the argument. In 1991 Richter came up with a way of synthesizing certain aspects of the glass panes and the mirrors and of highlighting the conciliatory nature of illusion and semblance. At his exhibition at the Anthony d'Offay Gallery in London he showed not only oil paintings but also a group of vertical format panes of glass, singly and in pairs, which were coated from behind with various pigments – grey, blood red, brown, blue, green, red.[45] Richter described these works as "glass that doesn't show the picture behind it but repeats – mirrors – what is in front of it. And in the case of the coloured mirrors, the result was a kind of cross between a monochrome painting and a mirror, a 'Neither/Nor' – which is what I like about it."[46] The ambiguousness of these works arises from the fact that they draw the viewer's gaze towards themselves only to instantly return it again, because there is nothing to be seen on their surfaces. The coating is behind the surface, inaccessible. There is nothing to catch the viewer's eye other than what is happening in the space in front of the coloured mirror.

That same year, in response to a commission from a bank in Düsseldorf, Richter designed a room with square coloured and clear mirrors.[47] However, these were installed as a frieze so high up above the windows

45 *Gerhard Richter: Mirrors*, exh. cat. London: Anthony d'Offay Gallery, 1991, nos. 28–32.

46 "Interview with Jonas Storsve" [1991], in *Text*, p. 272.

47 Elger 740.

in the foyer that people moving about in that space only saw reflected light in them – not themselves and other people. At floor level there were also six large, grey mirrors installed in niches in the wall, which silently bore witness to anything happening in that internal space.[48] That was the first appearance in Richter's work of the grey mirrors that would return a decade later in various configurations. In 2001 he created a group of eight vertical-format grey mirrors for the 21st Century Museum of Contemporary Art, Kanazawa, which are distributed evenly around the walls of a room; in 2002 he made a second group of eight grey mirrors for the Deutsche Guggenheim in Berlin – these mirrors could be variously tilted on their fixings.[49] These were followed in 2003 by a six-part series of pairs of grey mirrors, which combined to form squares; in 2014 Richter created a group of four asymmetrical, horizontal-format double mirrors in two different grey tones[50] and most recently – rather differently – two double mirrors for Münster.

These mirrors have an important precursor in the pair of grey mirrors that Richter conceived in 1992 for his

---

48 Elger 741. On this project, see *Oswald Mathias Ungers / Gerhard Richter / Sol LeWitt: Hypo-Bank, Niederlassung Düsseldorf, Königsallee 17*, Munich: Bayerische Hypotheken- und Wechsel-Bank Aktiengesellschaft, 1991.

49 Elger 874/1–8, 878/1–8. See the detailed documentation of the Berlin mirrors in *Gerhard Richter: Acht Grau*, exh. cat. Berlin Deutsche Guggenheim, 2002.

50 Elger 935/1–4.

picture cabinet at documenta IX.[51] This double mirror played the part of a wordless companion in amongst the paintings on display. At the same time the two mirrors, separated by a dark shadow, were mounted at a slight angle to the wall with the result that they did not directly confront the viewer with his or her likeness but instead reflected the diagonally opposite wall and the view out to the park. Visitors to the pendulum in the Dominican Church are not met by a situation where identical mirrors reflect each other. In fact the pairs of mirrors, with their subtle greys, differentiate the presence of reflections of the architecture, the pendulum, and people in the space. While the pendulum steadily swings, the mirrors reflect chance activities in the area around them differently because of their different grey hues. This explains why there had to be a pair of mirrors rather than a single mirror on each side wall (in the same way that in the work done in 1967 there were four panes of glass rather than just a single pane). A double mirror averts the impression of unambiguity that would be conveyed by a single reflective surface. A pair of reflective surfaces dislocates the viewer, whereas as a single surface would unequivocally locate him or her in a particular position.

And then there is also the pendulum bob, which Richter insisted must look like the previously mentioned stainless steel sphere. The bob with its highly polished surface is the third reflective object in the space; that and

---

51 Elger 765.

its constant motion make it impossible for the human eye to immediately take it in. Since the pendulum swings according to its own laws there is an uninterrupted flow of reflections between the moving sphere and the static double mirrors, with no need of any external input nor even of a viewer. The work accepts the viewer's presence, but does not require it.

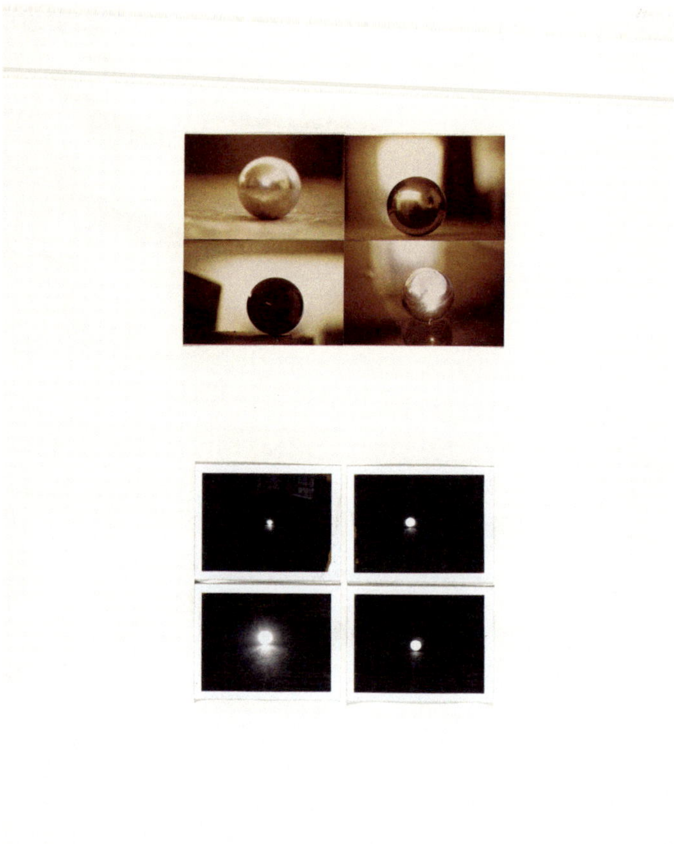

FIG. 50

Spheres, *Atlas*, sheet 81, 1968

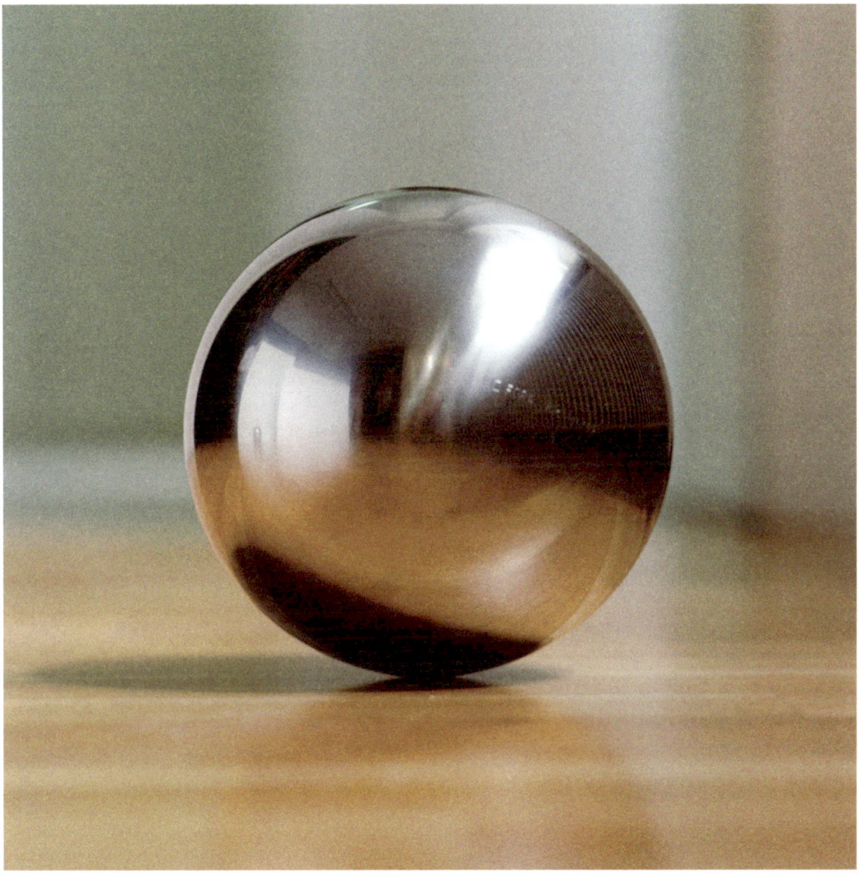

FIG. 51
Spheres III, 1992

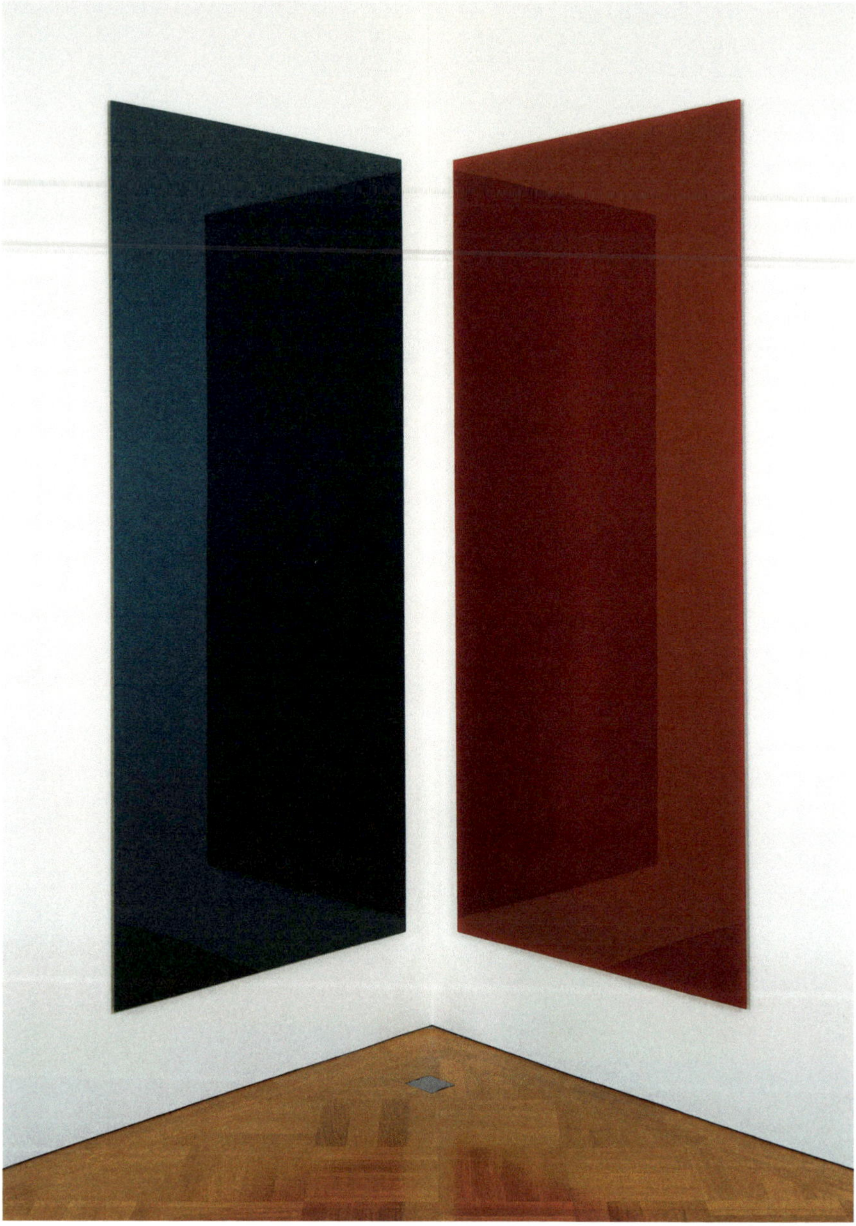

FIG. 52

Corner Mirror, Green-Red (737/2), 1991

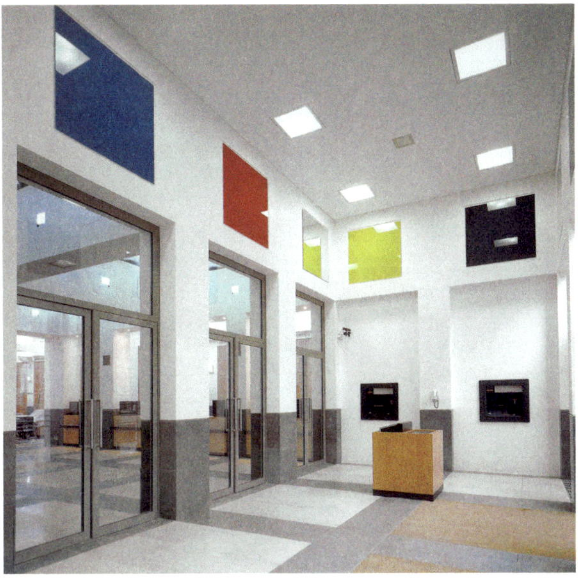

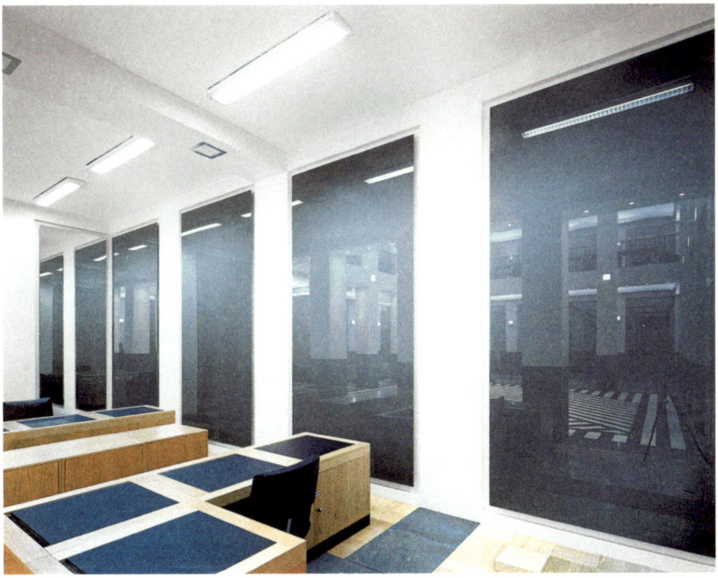

FIGS. 53 and 54

Twelve Mirrors for a Bank (740), 1991
Six Mirrors for a Bank (741), 1991

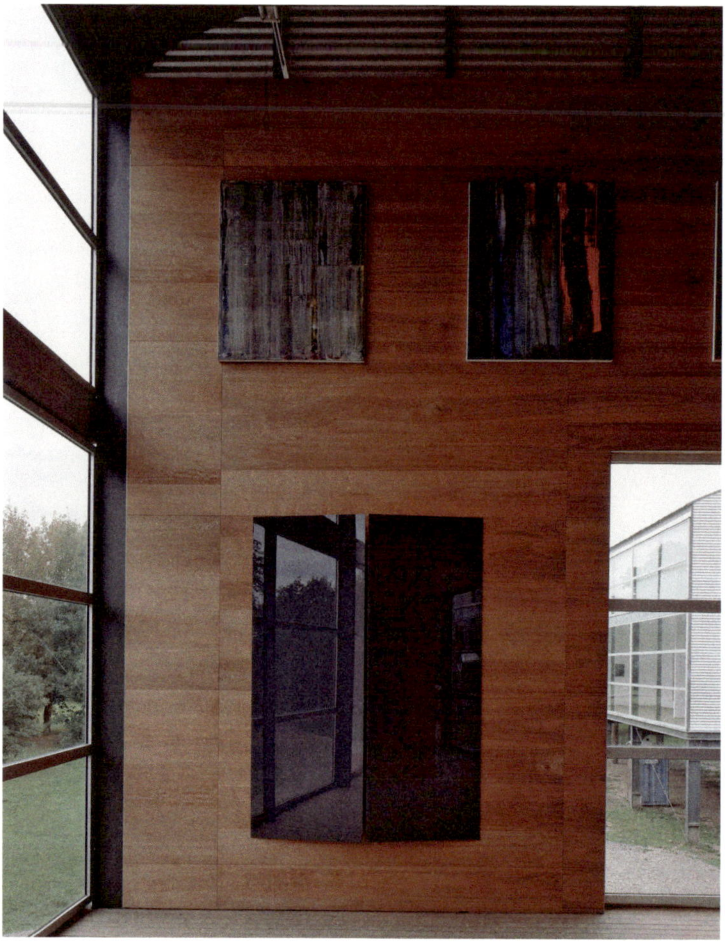

FIG. 55

Grey Mirror (765), 1992,
documenta IX, Kassel, 1992

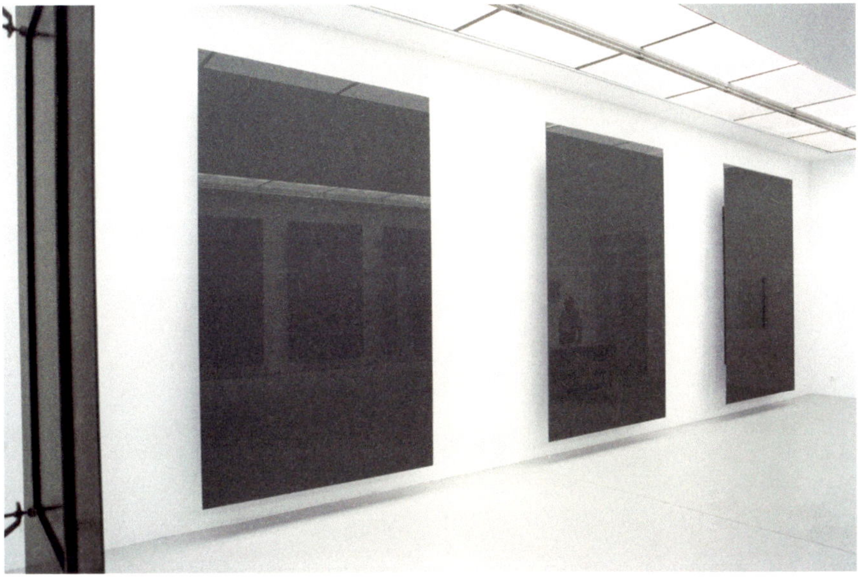

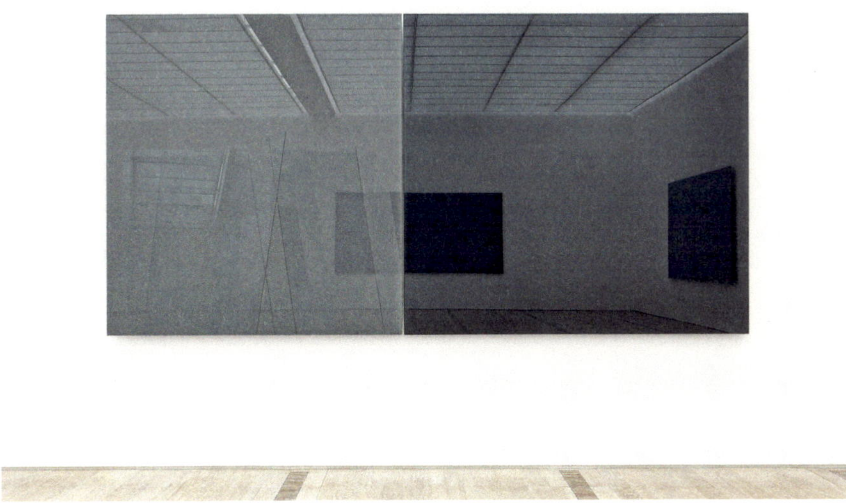

FIGS. 56 and 57

Eight Grey (874/1–8), 2001
Double Grey (935/1–4), 2014

FIG. 58

Two Greys Juxtaposed (143/1), 1966

Grey

As we have said, when Richter was working on his project for Münster he replaced coloured mirrors with grey mirrors. This is hardly surprising, because although there are a number of monochrome paintings in Richter's oeuvre, he has always kept his distance from the notion of monochromaticism as an artistic category in its own right, which certain painters signed up to in the 1980s. Richter never had any interest in monochromaticism as a celebration of colour or as the last throes of painting; monochromaticism only had meaning for him insofar as it depicted something. Thus the individual hues in his colour charts, such as *Ten Colours* (1966),[52] are not autonomous phenomena but rather neutral samples, and in the case of the coloured mirrors mentioned earlier here, Richter used those monochromes as an ambivalent vehicle for reflecting viewers and the space. Richter also started to work on his Grey Paintings in 1966 – not as a continuation of his previous use of black-and-white photographs as the basis of oil paintings, but as representations of the colour grey. The first of these grey paintings were called *Two Greys Juxtaposed*, *Two Greys, One upon the Other*, and *Three Greys,*

52 Elger 135-1.

One upon the Other.[53] Within a year Richter did a number of smaller grey paintings, with variously textured surfaces – as opposed to the neutral surfaces of the first group. These would then be followed in the 1970s by more grey paintings in wall-sized formats. He commented on that choice of colour in an interview, consistently defining it *ex negativo*: "I did have a special relationship with grey. Grey, to me, was absence of opinion, nothing, neither/nor. It was also a means of manifesting my own relationship with apparent reality. I didn't want to say: 'It is thus and not otherwise.' And then perhaps I didn't want anyone to confuse the pictures with reality."[54]

Richter's engagement with this non-motif came to a climax in 1975 in his creation of a room with eight identical grey paintings for the Städtisches Museum Mönchengladbach.[55] This series of intentionally identical paintings was designed to dispel the notion all too easily conveyed by a single grey painting that it was only there as a foil for the representational paintings. It was only in that self-contained spatial situation that the grey paintings achieved their goal of total disinterest, the antithesis to opinion, statement, and subjective presence. At the same time, the grey paintings were not to overwhelm the viewer by virtue of their presence in the space, because they did not embody the idea of the negation of every positive

---

53 Elger 143/1–3.

54 "Interview with Peter Sager" [1972], in *Text*, p. 67.

55 Elger 367/1-8.

quality – they were merely a representation, a symbol of that idea: "Grey. It makes no statement whatever; it evokes neither feelings nor associations; it is really neither visible or invisible. Its inconspicuousness gives it the capacity to mediate, to make visible, in a positively illusionistic way, like a photograph. It has the capacity that no other colour has, to make 'nothing' visible."[56]

With the two grey double mirrors flanking the pendulum, the scientific fact is multiply replicated – by each individual mirrored surface – and turned into an image, not just once but many times. The fact is present, but at the same time it is also an image, as opposed to the grey paintings that – since they represent "nothing" – do display their factual side. The pendulum as an image between grey images or the pendulum as a fact between equally factual images: all other combinations of image and fact are contained within that.

---

56 "From a letter to Edy de Wilde, 23 February 1975", in *Text*, p. 92.

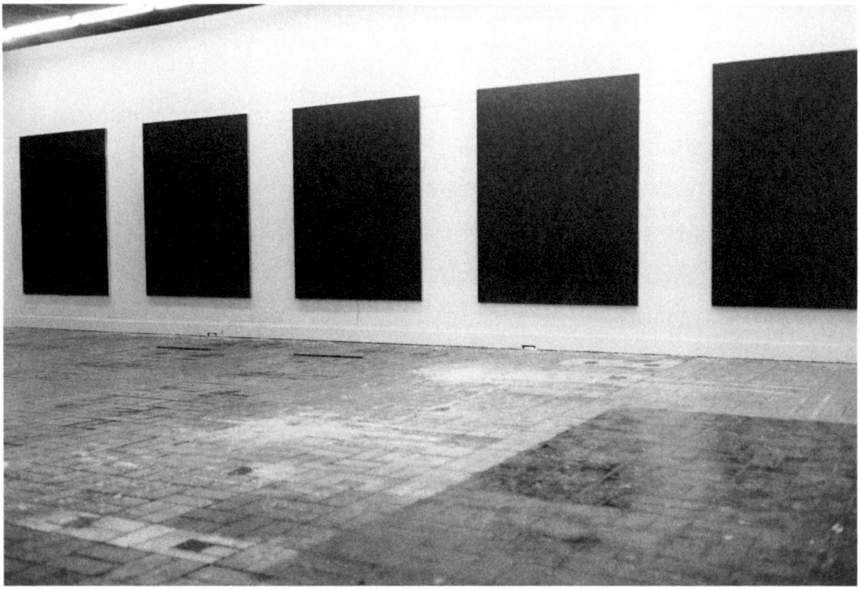

FIG. 59

Grey (367/1–8), 1975

Pictorial Spaces

Although we have come full circle to Richter's work for Münster, one topic is still left untouched, namely "art in architecture", or rather, architecture defined by art. This also has a long history in Richter's work. In 1970–71 Richter made a series of studies of imaginary rooms with either entire or partial picture walls.[57] In an interview Richter once remarked "Oh yes, that is such a dream of mine – that the pictures will become an environment or become architecture; that would be even more effective."[58] The rooms in these studies are deftly suggested with just a few steeply-angled lines of perspective, heightening their drama, and the pictures are pasted-in photographs. The rooms themselves are austere, some with classical ornamentation framing the images; miniscule figures in some of the rooms indicate that the architecture is monumental in its dimensions. There are rooms with pictures of clouds, mountains, oceans – heroic landscapes, one might say. Elsewhere there are gigantic enlargements of some of Richter's colour streaks. Individual images either fill an entire wall or are inserted into fields on the walls; whatever

57 Illustrated in *Atlas*, pp. 212, 218–52.

58 "Interview with Dorothea Dietrich" [1985], in *Text*, p. 154.

the case they respond to the idea of pictorial décor in interiors with pathos formulas that have an impact, which is at least equal, or even superior, to that of the architecture. Speculations of this kind are relatively rare in Richter's work, which adds particular interest to these studies, which would later come menacingly to life again in Thomas Schütte's picture panels. Richter is dreaming here of the totality of a pictorial presence, as it were a reversal of the comprehensive reflections of the sphere; anyone entering one of those fictive rooms has no option but to succumb to the totality of the images. However, in Richter's case no message, no ideology is purveyed by this pictorial world. The clouds and landscape details only communicate their own monumentality. They fill the rooms yet also signal their emptiness – they represent an artistic dream of overwhelming power and beauty that appears to be under its own spell. Richter's ideas have something in common with French revolutionary architecture, which was not designed for a ruler but as a representation of an abstract absolute. That form of abstraction is a fitting counterpart for an artist who disappears as a persona and now only adopts a symbolic stance through the oeuvre he has created.

Richter has, however, rarely had the chance to realize his dream of rooms of that kind. One of the first, which came at around the same time as he made the studies, was the room for portrait heads of Palermo and Richter that the two artists designed for an exhibition at Galerie Heiner Friedrich in Cologne in 1971.[59] Although the walls are not

59 Elger 297-1 and 297-2.

occupied by images, the combination of painted walls and figures ensues from a similar notion of the indissoluble continuum of the space and the work presented in it. Richter did, however, achieve something closer to those studies in his design for the installation of his retrospective at Kunsthalle Düsseldorf in 1971 where he used landscapes and cloud pictures to create an overwhelming spatial impact.[60] This was then followed by his concept for the central room in the German Pavilion at the Venice Biennale, for which he painted 48 portraits of leading figures from the early twentieth century.[61] And there is a more recent example of this notion in Richter's enamelled glass painting in black, red, and gold for the entrance hall of the German Reichstag in Berlin; at over 20 metres tall this painting far exceeds the usual dimensions of Richter's paintings. Lastly, Richter's interest in creating series arose from his desire to transform a room into a clearly defined situation by means of paintings. During the painting process compositions that are closely related in terms of either their form or content progressively form a self-contained ensemble that takes possession of the walls in the artist's studio; subsequently, at least for a limited time when the series is presented in a gallery or a museum there is hope of establishing a valid connection with the means of painting.

---

60 The exhibition plan is published in *Gerhard Richter: Arbeiten 1962 bis 1971,* exh. cat. Düsseldorf: Kunstverein für die Rheinlande und Westfalen, 1971, unpaginated. The sketches illustrated on p. 245 of *Atlas* refer to Kunsthalle Düsseldorf.

61 Elger 324/1–48. See also *Atlas*, p. 41.

However, any such exhibitions are only temporary and the quality of the architectural setting is unpredictable. The painting at the Reichstag is a permanent installation, but it is entirely solitary. It is therefore hardly surprising that when Richter first visited the Dominican Church he was delighted to find the perfect location for a work of art that was yet to be made – a classical Baroque space with columns, walls divided into different sections, and a dome – in every sense the opposite to the functionalist industrial structure that had initially been up for discussion. His encounter with this new set of circumstances allowed him to imagine an ensemble in a space that not only houses it but in fact sustains it in such a way that the ongoing interplay of three elements that relate to each other is so clear and convincing that nothing more is needed. Anyone entering the church and seeing the work of art takes it as written that this is how everything was and always will be.

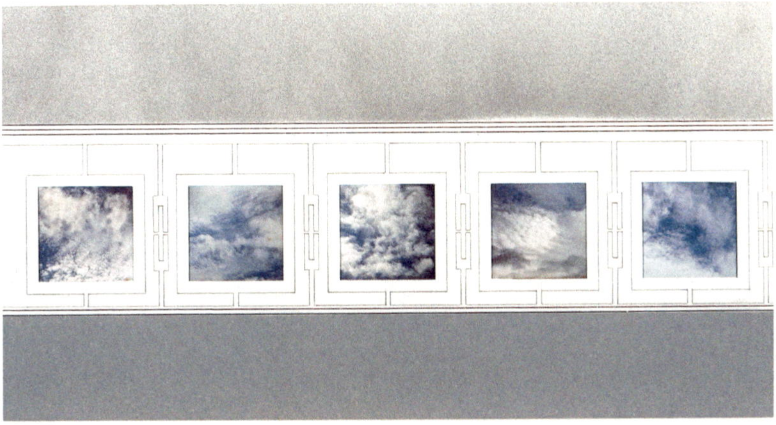

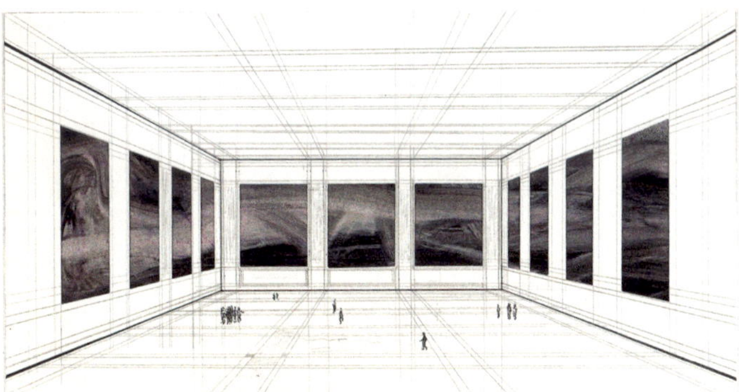

FIGS. 60 and 61

Rooms, *Atlas*, sheets 229 and 234, 1971

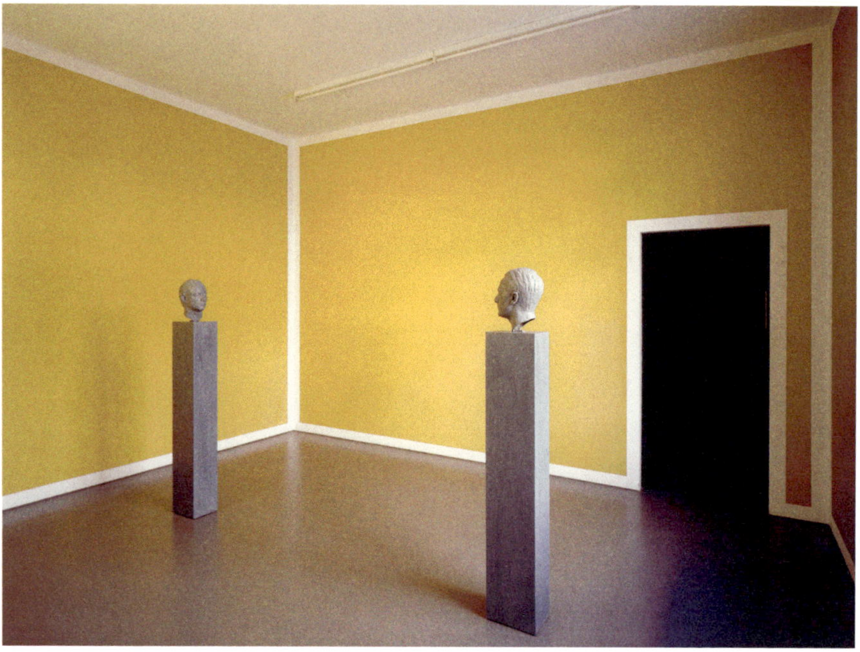

FIG. 62

Two Sculptures for a Room by Palermo (297/2), 1971. Installation in the Städtische Galerie im Lenbachhaus, München

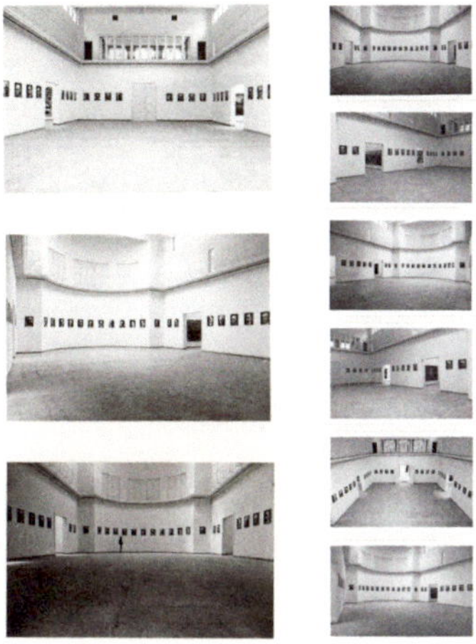

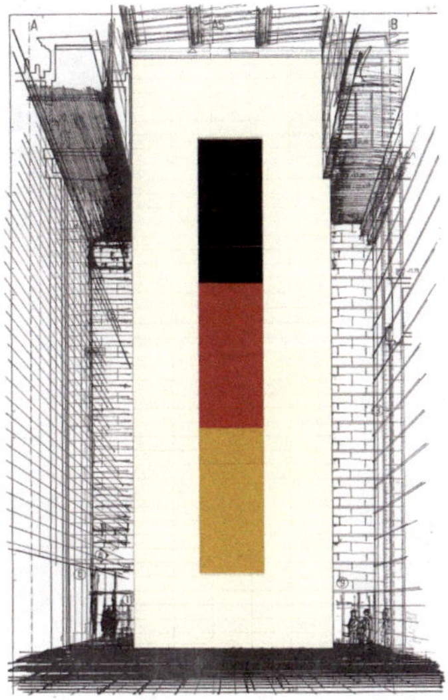

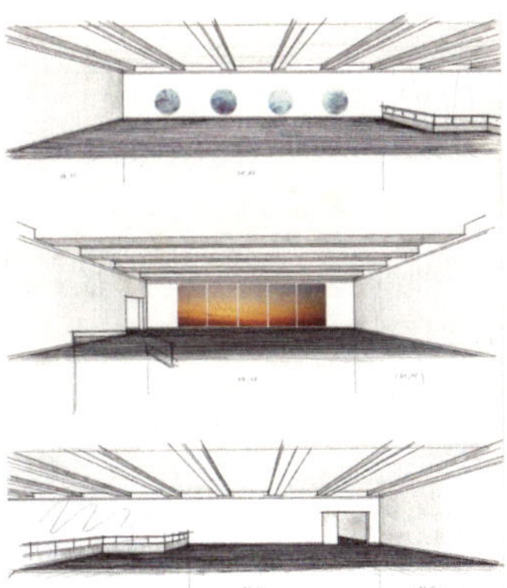

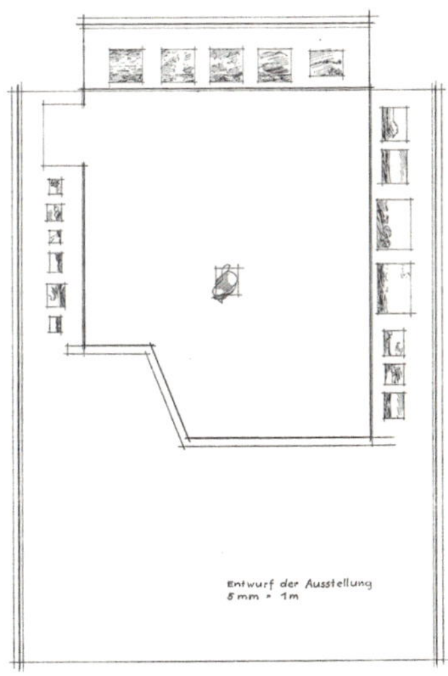

FIGS. 63–66

48 Portraits, *Atlas*, sheet 41, 1971. Reichstag, *Atlas*, sheet 655, 1998
Räume (Kunsthalle Düsseldorf), 1971, *Atlas*, sheet 245, 1971
Installation diagram, Kunsthalle Düsseldorf, 1971

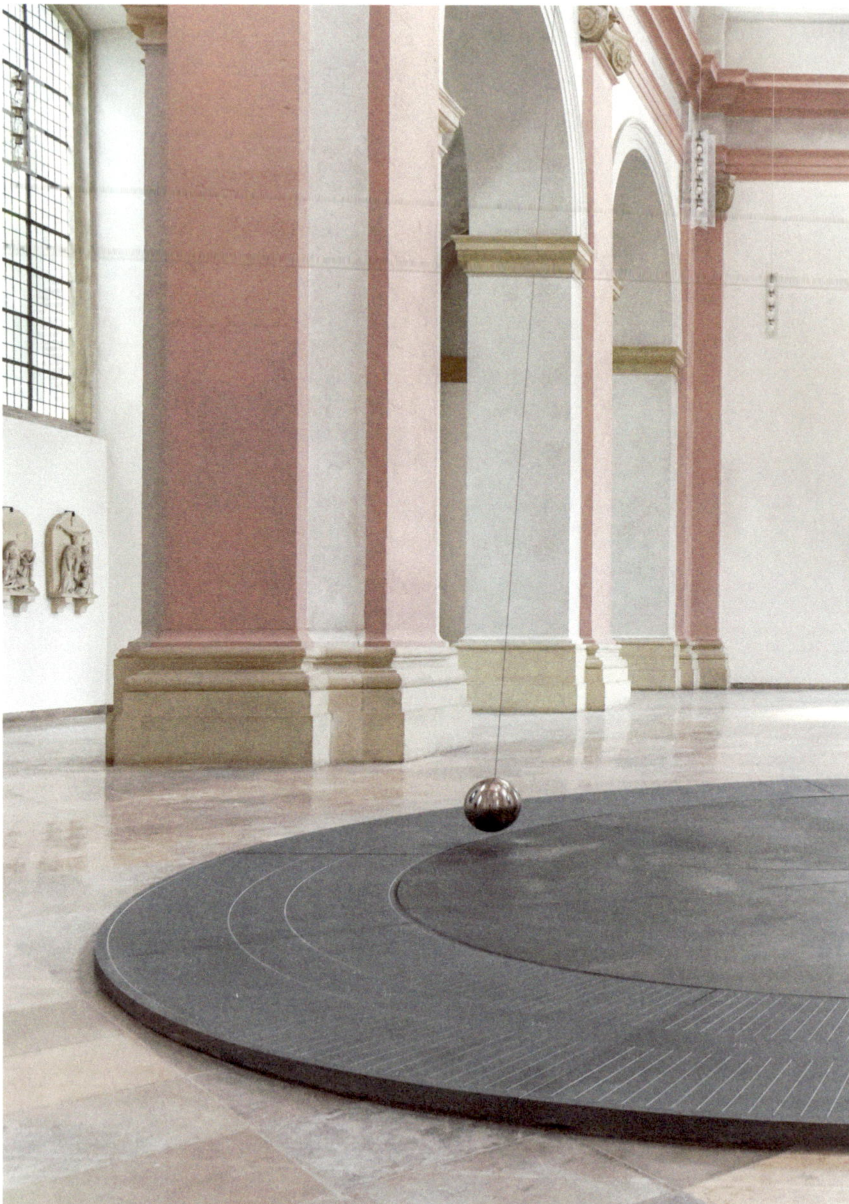

FIG. 67
Pendulum in the Dominikanerkirche, 2018

Two Grey Double Mirrors for a Pendulum (953)

Richter's work for Münster in fact serves as a succinct, unexpected résumé covering certain fundamental aspects of his art. For one thing, there is the juxtaposition of scientific fact and artistic invention, which could also be read the other way round, that is to say, as the juxtaposition of scientific findings and artistic fact. There is the regularity of the oscillating pendulum compared to the unforeseeable, fleeting images in the mirrors, or, as one might also say, the constant rotation of the world around the pendulum and the mirrors' uninterrupted reflection of the same static, spatial situation. And there is the light that enters through the windows at ground level and through the clerestory and falls on the swinging, reflecting sphere, and the grey of the mirrors that mutes and returns that light and forms a quiet zone on the walls. Elements that enter the ensemble as facts coalesce into a work of art in the context created by Gerhard Richter. The pendulum and the double mirrors are not like paintings in an exhibition or a museum collection, which could always be replaced by others; on the contrary they complement the ecclesiastical architecture, which derives its own sense of order from the fact that it makes the connection between the work of art and its visitors.

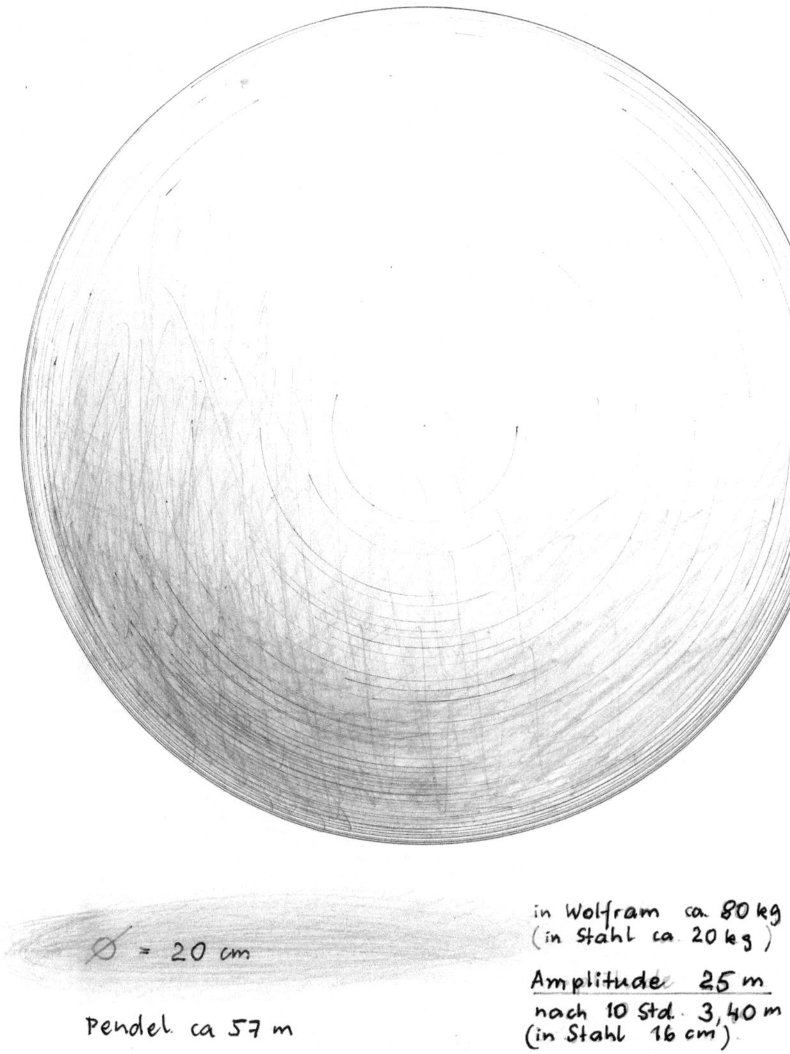

FIG. 68

Drawing for a pendulum bob, 2017

The author thanks

Gerhard Richter

Atelier Richter: Konstanze Ell

Stadt Münster: Cornelia Wilkens, Dr Gail Kirkpatrick, Marcus Lutkemeyer

Städtische Galerie im Lenbachhaus, Munich: Matthias Mühling, Direktor; Sarah Bock, Sammlungsarchiv

Kasper König, Berlin

Photo Credits

Unless otherwise stated: Gerhard Richter, Cologne

Deutsches Museum, Munich, Archiv (BN_59254): p. 9

Fondation Beyeler, Riehen / Basel: p. 93

Holt/Smithson Foundation, Santa Fe, New Mexico: p. 63

MICHAEL C. MOELLER, Münster: Cover design (front and back), pp. 2, 4, 49, 50, 106, 111

© 2021. Digital Image, The Museum of Modern Art, New York / SCALA, Florence; © Association Marcel Duchamp / VG Bild-Kunst, Bonn 2021: p. 57

Presseamt Münster: p. 6

Gerhard Richter, Cologne: pp. 13, 20, 21, 26, 27, 32, 39

S.M.A.K., Ghent / Dirk Pauwels: pp. 69, 76

Dieter Schwarz, Zurich: p. 38

Städtische Galerie im Lenbachhaus, Munich / Simone Gänsheimer, Ernst Jank: pp. 40–45, 65, 88, 102, 104, 105

Nic Tenwiggenhorn, Berlin: p. 91

Wako Works of Art, Tokyo / Keizo Kioku: p. 79

Wako Works of Art, Tokyo / Takahiro Igarashi: p. 78

Wikipedia / Florian Adler, 2010: p. 28

Wikipedia / Rémih, 2011: p. 10

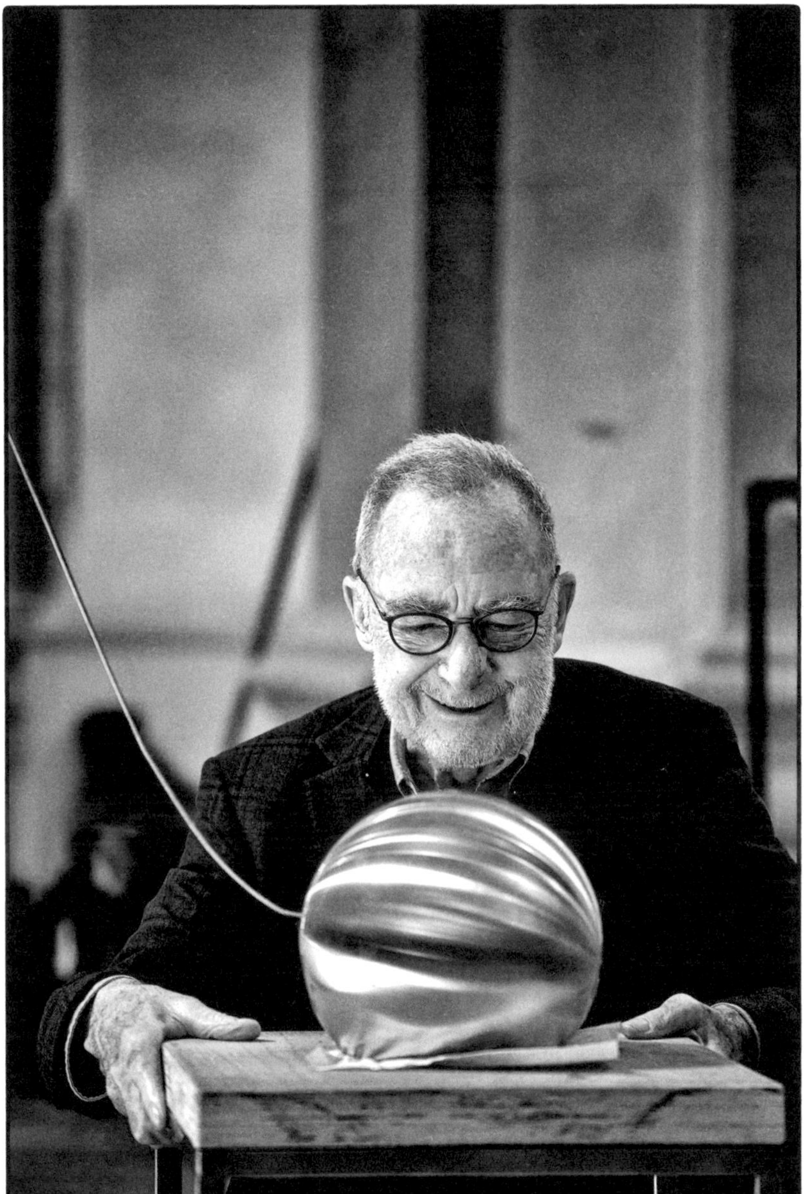

Writings of the Gerhard Richter Archive Dresden, Volume 20
Edited by Dietmar Elger

Translation: Fiona Elliott

Design: Silke Fahnert, Uwe Koch, Cologne

Lithography: Gundula Seraphin, Bad Münstereifel

Production: DZA Druckerei zu Altenburg GmbH

Published by

Verlag der Buchhandlung Walther und Franz König, Köln
Ehrenstraße 4, D-50672 Köln

and

Staatliche Kunstsammlungen Dresden, Gerhard Richter Archiv
Albertinum / Tzschirnerplatz 2
D-01067 Dresden
TEL. +49 (0)351 4914 7770
EMAIL: gra@skd.museum
www. gerhard-richter-archiv.de

Bibliographic information published by the Deutschen Nationalbibliothek

The Deutsche Nationalbibliothek lists this publication in the Deutsche Nationalbibliografie; detailed bibliographic data are available in the Internet at http://dnb.d-nb.de.

Printed in Germany

Distribution

Buchhandlung Walther König
Ehrenstraße 4, D-50672 Köln
Tel.: +49 (0) 221 – 20 59 653
verlag@buchhandlung-walther-koenig.de

ISBN 978-3-7533-0026-9

Gefördert durch

Freistaat SACHSEN

Staatliche Kunstsammlungen Dresden

IN DER SAMMLUNGSTRADITION DES HAUSES WETTIN A.L.